ASSEMBLAGE THEORY AND AFFECT

ASSEMBLAGE THEORY AND AFFECT

Ian Buchanan

BLOOMSBURY ACADEMIC
LONDON • NEW YORK • OXFORD • NEW DELHI • SYDNEY

BLOOMSBURY ACADEMIC
Bloomsbury Publishing Plc, 50 Bedford Square, London, WC1B 3DP, UK
Bloomsbury Publishing Inc, 1359 Broadway, New York, NY 10018, USA
Bloomsbury Publishing Ireland, 29 Earlsfort Terrace, Dublin 2, D02 AY28, Ireland

BLOOMSBURY, BLOOMSBURY ACADEMIC and the Diana logo are
trademarks of Bloomsbury Publishing Plc

First published in Great Britain 2026

Copyright © Ian Buchanan, 2026

Ian Buchanan has asserted his right under the Copyright, Designs and
Patents Act, 1988, to be identified as Author of this work.

For legal purposes the Acknowledgements on p. viii constitute an
extension of this copyright page.

Cover image © Sylverarts / AdobeStock

Bloomsbury Publishing Plc does not have any control over, or responsibility for,
any third-party websites referred to or in this book. All internet addresses given
in this book were correct at the time of going to press. The author and publisher
regret any inconvenience caused if addresses have changed or sites have ceased
to exist, but can accept no responsibility for any such changes.

A catalogue record for this book is available from the British Library.

A catalog record for this book is available from the Library of Congress.

ISBN: HB: 978-1-3502-6876-0
       PB: 978-1-3502-6877-7
       ePDF: 978-1-3502-6878-4
       eBook: 978-1-3502-6879-1

Typeset by RefineCatch Limited, Bungay, Suffolk
Printed and bound in Great Britain

For product safety related questions contact productsafety@bloomsbury.com.

To find out more about our authors and books visit www.bloomsbury.com
and sign up for our newsletters.

For David Savat

CONTENTS

ACKNOWLEDGEMENTS

I wrote this book in the strange interregnum between the expected end of the Trump era and its unexpected return that will perhaps be known as the 'Biden years' if anyone can forgot the horror of Gaza that Biden did nothing to stop and for which he cannot be exonerated. It was begun in a relatively safe corner of the world during a global pandemic that took the lives of millions of people and disrupted the lives of everyone. The events of the pandemic years (2020–2) will no doubt be studied forensically for decades to come, but for those of us who lived through it I think it is important to remember just how baffling the experience was for most of the time.

I began writing as Trump's presidency was coming to an end and to be honest I did not believe I would ever see him back in the White House and yet here we are. As I was finishing this book, I was appalled to see the world stand by and let people die in their thousands in Gaza at the hands of the Israeli military. The shame of this stains the entirety of humanity as Deleuze once put it speaking of the Holocaust.

These events have shaped this book, directly and indirectly, by constantly foregrounding the problem of how to explain human action. In my view, that is the central mission of schizoanalysis. To the extent that the various forms of so-called new materialism sideline the problem of desire they render schizoanalysis apolitical and unable to continue its mission and should therefore be rigorously rejected.

This was not an easy book to write and I am hopeful that the finished text does not bear the traces of the difficulty I had writing it. In the preface to *Difference and Repetition*, which was part of Deleuze's submission for his *Doctorat d'État*, he writes: 'To satisfy ignorance is to put off writing until tomorrow – or, rather, to make it impossible.' I can honestly say I've never felt more keenly the truth of that observation than I did with the writing of this book, which was often written from a point of ignorance that only much later became a point of illumination. It took me a long time to let go of certain preconceptions I had when I started writing this book, but once I did I found myself on an intellectual rollercoaster ride that was as disconcerting as it was exciting.

The difficulty of writing this book was compounded by the soul-crushing turbulence of working through several rounds of so-called change management in my place of employment. I can honestly say universities in Australia are no longer recognizable to me as places of learning. The barbarians are no longer at the gate, they're in the citadel, and everything we once held dear as academics is burning.

This book was explicitly conceived as sequel to *Assemblage Theory and Method* (2021). Unlike my previous books it was initially written in isolation from the community of Deleuze and Guattari scholars that for three decades has sustained and stimulated me to continue my explorations of Deleuze and Guattari's work. Fortunately, as the final draft was coming together the travel restrictions of the Covid years were eased and I was able to test drive sections of it in front of an actual audience. The *Deleuze and Guattari Studies* conferences in Prague (online), Seoul (online), Belgrade, Delft and Taipei were a godsend in this regard.

I also want to acknowledge a deep and abiding intellectual and personal debt to Fredric Jameson who passed away in 2024. To my mind, he was and remains the most insightful reader of Deleuze and Guattari in any language and I find his work a constant source of inspiration and a powerful resource for prompting me to think differently. I highly recommend his final book, *The Years of Theory*, as a starting point for anyone interested in contextualizing Deleuze and Guattari's thought in their historical and intellectual milieu (as one always should).

I benefited greatly from conversations with Ciara Cremin, Claire Colebrook, Chantelle Gray, Glen Fuller, Tauel Harper, Patricio Landaeta, Cate Montes, Chris Mueller, Tess Lea, David Savat, Natascha Schmelz, Sam Sellar, Joseph Schaal, Janae Sholtz, Marcelo Svirsky, Greg Thompson and Gordon Waitt. My PhD students, Daniel Cheney, Tom Fisher, Georgia Gibbs, Marc Haas, William Wentworth and Zhifei Xiang, have been a constant inspiration to try to produce a 'useful' version of Deleuze and Guattari's work. Last, I must thank my long-suffering editor Liza Thompson for her unwavering support and belief.

I dedicate this book to David Savat. Our adventures together have been legendary, long may they continue.

Wombarra, 2025

INTRODUCTION

[A] commentary should act as a veritable double and bear the maximal modification appropriate to a double. (One imagines a philosophically bearded Hegel, a philosophically clean-shaven Marx, in the same way as a moustached Mona Lisa.)[1]

In what follows, for better or worse, I have tried to embrace this maxim demanding maximal modification as fully possible. The account of Deleuze and Guattari's concept of affect found here will not follow the usual course one finds in affect theory. Similarly, the account of the concept of the assemblage found here does not follow the usual course one finds in assemblage theory. This is perhaps not unexpected since it extends and deepens the work I began in *Assemblage Theory and Method*. The combination of affect and assemblage is likewise perhaps unexpected, but I have come to think it is necessary. This book tries to do three things: first, it wants to make an argument about the way Deleuze and Guattari conceive of affect; second, it wants to make an argument about how certain of Deleuze and Guattari's concepts should be handled; and third, it wants to do both these things in a manner and in a style of language that requires only minimal familiarity with the work of Deleuze and Guattari. Of the three, the last objective proved the most difficult to achieve and I wouldn't want to say whether I have been successful or not. In the interests of clarity, I thought it might be helpful to offer a summary of my arguments from the outset. I tend to share Jameson's concern about the perils of premature clarification, but I also acknowledge that delayed clarification can be frustrating.

The premise of the argument I intend to present here can be stated very simply. *Affect is a function of desire* – its powers are the powers we attribute to desire. As such, like desire it should be considered a psychical agency. This corrects what I take to be an error in affect theory's take-up of Deleuze and Guattari, namely the treatment of affect as though it is separate from and not directly related to desire. I also argue that insofar as it is a function of desire it is involuntary. As a psychical agency, *affect is a capacitating power* – it empowers us to meet life. This reorients our understanding of desire around questions to do with 'being able to' do something instead of the assumed 'wanting to' do something. Affect, I argue, cannot be adequately accounted for in terms of a stimulus and response framework as is generally the case in affect theory. Affect is not the measure of our response to a given stimulus, it is rather the capacity we have to respond to a stimulus in the way that we do. This can be seen in the way affect tends to be experienced as enduring rather than fleeting. We tend to think people whose affect varies on a rapid cycle are 'unstable' and perhaps in need of medication. One definition of 'normal' would be an ongoing and stable capacity to face the day every day without fear, doubt, paranoia or anxiety, causing us to become stuck. All of these symptoms are, I want to suggest, disturbances in our affect, in our capacity to meet the day.

This is, I would argue, the essential argument of Deleuze and Guattari's schizoanalytic project which, as many people have recognized – intuited is probably a better word – without necessarily acknowledging, is underpinned by a therapeutic framework that is a kind of survivor's guide to late capitalism. The concept of the rhizome, which is first and foremost a therapeutic notion, illustrates this point perfectly. The rhizome is a lifeline – if you're stuck in a dark place, i.e. if your affect is so flattened you can't get out of bed, then latch onto something, anything, and change your situation by finding a way out of the darkness. This is a matter of the capacity to do, rather than a particular kind of feeling, though it is often the case that the latter masks the former.

Building on the premise stated above that affect is a psychical agency that determines our capacity to meet the day, my argument has four steps (taken directly from Deleuze and Guattari's work, although not stepped out in the manner I will present it here). The first step is the claim that the assemblage, body without organs and the abstract machine are components of affect. The second step is the claim that the totality of the bodies without organs and the totality of abstract machines constitute the plane of immanence and the plane of organization, respectively, and these two planes are the principal dimensions of our affect. The third step is the claim that the specific nature of our affect, which is to say its capacitating power, depends upon the particular combinations of bodies without organs and abstract machines that we have been able to put together by means of the assemblages available to us. I will refer to this final step as the problem of the composition of affect. This brings us to the fourth and final step, which is the claim that the fabrication of a plane of immanence and a plane of organization by means of assemblages that works for us is the ultimate goal of all our mental activity. This is what Deleuze means by an ethics of desire.

In reality, this last claim falls into the category of an absolute presupposition since the entirety of schizoanalysis hinges on it, but one only sees its necessity when one has followed the previous steps. This is doubtless because of Deleuze's loathing of so-called first principles, but for those of us interested in developing a model of critical analysis based on schizoanalysis it is the keystone needed to make everything fit together. The incomplete project of schizoanalysis Deleuze and Guattari initiated is – I would say – *essentially concerned* with understanding the various ways and means people have of making or otherwise finding their way to a state of affect that works for them. This is not always easy or possible and in many cases people find themselves stuck on a body without organs that does not combine well with other bodies without organs and therefore inhibits the formation of a plane of immanence. Similarly they may find themselves constricted by an overly rigid abstract machine they cannot unbuckle enough to find breathing space. In both cases, it is always the task of the assemblage to rectify this situation, but there are no guarantees.

Unified Field Theory

There is one crucial difficulty concerning Deleuze and Guattari's work on affect that needs to be addressed at the outset. And that is the somewhat embarrassing fact that there is no straightforward answer anywhere in their work to the question, 'What is affect?' Indeed, there are several answers to this question, i.e. several different concepts of affect, none of which are fully in agreement with the other. I will explore the specifics of the different versions of affect found in Deleuze and Guattari's work in Chapter 4, but for now I just want to note that this is, of course, an untenable theoretical position. So, I am going to present a case for what might be called, borrowing from Jameson, a unified field theory approach to affect.[2] While this nod to physics is deliberate it should not be taken literally. It functions only as inspiration for the approach I want to take, which seeks to build a coherent model of affect from an apparently disparate and at times divergent set of ideas and applications in Deleuze and Guattari's work. As Deleuze put it,

> Of course, we realize the dangers of citing scientific propositions outside of their own sphere. It is the danger of arbitrary metaphor or of forced application. But perhaps these dangers are averted if we restrict ourselves to taking from scientific operators a particular conceptualizable character which itself refers to non-scientific areas, and converges with science without applying it or making it a metaphor.[3]

Guattari is very clear about what it means to take inspiration from science, which he and Deleuze frequently do, and the value in doing so. For example, in a beautiful passage in the posthumously published collection *Lines of Flight*, he says rather than 'clinging to simplistic modes of causality' we should 'take inspiration from more recent "models" [i.e. quantum physics]', but then adds a crucial caveat: 'Inspiration has to be understood here in the poetic sense or that of walkers who need a change of scenery.' It is not, he says, 'a matter of proposing new tracings, or the compulsive search for a "scientificity" in these domains – something that seems to arise more from obsessional neurosis than from a theoretical analysis connected with social realities.'[4] The turn to science, particularly cognitive science, has, I think, also occasioned, albeit unintentionally, a turn away from philosophy in general and Deleuze and Guattari's work in particular. I want to try to set that right by using science as a 'change of scenery' rather than a point of reference and propose an answer to the question 'What is affect?' that takes into account the full spectrum, i.e. the unified field of Deleuze and Guattari's work.

The unified field theory approach is intended to solve a set of practical difficulties which can be enumerated as follows. The first, and undoubtedly the most troubling, is the fact that Deleuze and Guattari do not always use the word 'affect' when they are talking about affect – e.g. becoming, haecceities, intensity, signs and flow are all used in place of affect – which of course raises the question of whether they are using several words for the same thing, or whether they are all different things (I answer this question in the next section). Second, they appear not use the word 'affect' in a consistent manner – sometimes it refers to what a body can do, and at other times the discharge of emotion, and to really confuse matters it is also used to refers to physical objects such as jewels and the different attributes of swords. This in turn raises the question of whether or not affect can sensibly refer to such a range of apparently different things. Third, there is an always problematic distinction to be drawn between 'affect' and 'affects'. In most cases, 'affects' can be construed as corresponding to the particulate form, if you will, of 'affect', but this only makes sense to the extent one can settle on a definition of affect, which is far from straightforward.

There are, in a sense, only two ways forward: either there is an abstract form of affect which can account for the diversity of uses, or we need to take a differential approach and make some hard decisions about which is and which isn't the true form of 'affect'. Both of these approaches can be found in Deleuze and Guattari's work, so we cannot look to their work for guidance as to which is the 'right' path to take. For better or worse I am taking the first option; it is, I believe, both plausible and possible to theorize an abstract form of affect that can account for Deleuze and Guattari's terminological heterogeneity and explain its necessity.[5]

Jameson uses this unified field theory approach in his work, particularly *Marxism and Form*, to contend with Marxism's terminological inconsistencies which in many ways mirror what we face here. It works, he says, by subsuming 'apparently antagonistic or incommensurable critical operations, assigning them an undoubted sectoral validity within itself, and thus at once cancelling and preserving them'.[6] Although Deleuze's antipathy to dialectics is well known it is not at all clear that he would oppose a dialectical construction of this type because it does not follow the model he loathed of thesis, antithesis and synthesis, which Jameson rightly describes as a caricature in any case. Indeed, in Jameson's hands, the dialectic is a code phrase for a problematic, which according to Deleuze is where philosophy should begin.

In this instance, the problematic at hand is how to resolve the inconsistencies in Deleuze and Guattari's usage of 'affect' without having to either blunt the sharp edges of their differences and declare them null, or else adjudicate between them and determine which iteration of affect is the 'correct' one. Jameson's model solves this problem by subsuming all the differences under a single umbrella term that grants them 'sectoral validity' and places them all on equal footing as antagonistic parts of a greater multidimensional whole. The reason I think Deleuze and Guattari would not be opposed to this approach is that it is exactly the same approach they take in constructing the plane of immanence and the plane of organization. Each plane, as the totality of bodies without organs or abstract machines, is itself an 'untranscendable horizon' (to use Jameson's signature phrase) which grants its components 'sectoral validity'.

The plane of immanence and the plane of organization, which are essentially opposite sides of the same coin, together constitute an 'untranscendable horizon' in Deleuze and Guattari's work: there are no concepts that come before them in the sense of being necessarily presupposed – these are the terms Deleuze positions as absolute presuppositions – and there are no terms that come after them that would be capable of subsuming them. From the perspective of thought itself, then, affect is an 'untranscendable horizon'. My suggestion here is that in order to avoid the terminological difficulties we quickly find ourselves in if we try to adhere closely to the disparate ways Deleuze and Guattari use the term we need to situate them within a larger framework such as I have done.

On *Not* Getting Lost in Translation

Before concluding this overly long introduction, I want to add a few words about the way I have approached the third aspect of my project here, namely the explication of Deleuze and Guattari's concepts. Deleuze and Guattari's writing style is such that one cannot avoid the question – indeed, the problem – of how one should read their work. Certainly, in my case, it is a problem I find myself returning to time and again. This question, and the self-reflexion it occasions, is particularly important, I believe, when it comes to trying to define Deleuze and Guattari's concepts in such a way that we do not – as Jameson once put it (borrowing from Thurber) – end up drawing our own eye.[7] As a general rule, when I develop definitions of Deleuze and Guattari's concepts I try to avoid assuming prior knowledge of their work, or worse still resorting to using their own terms to define their terms.

I have always thought that Deleuze and Guattari's terminology should be approached as translations of terms that originated in a language (philosophical, psychological, psychoanalytic or even scientific) they no longer wish (us) to speak. The most obvious instance of this is the concept of the assemblage, which Guattari explicitly defined as a reworking of the Freudian notion of the complex.[8] There are at least two reasons why they might want us to set aside a particular conceptual language. The first, most obvious, but also least interesting reason is the well-known fact that some things can be said in one language, but not another, so changing languages is a matter of simple necessity.[9] This only becomes interesting to the degree that an author tries to find the means of saying what can't be said in a given language without changing languages – that is the scenario Deleuze and Guattari refer to as minor literature. The other reason has to do with a kind of conceptual censorship, or a refusal of certain kinds of political entanglement. I tend to think that this reason applies more than the first reason, but both are undoubtedly factors.

One might see Deleuze and Guattari's approach of inventing new words for old terms as an alternative to Derrida's solution to the same problem which he tried to resolve by writing things 'under erasure' (*sous rature*), a strategy he adapted from Heidegger which acknowledges the existence of a prior formulation of a given concept or idea, but also refuses to use it in the form that it was given.[10] In this way the impossibility of resolving the inherent flaws in the concept are nevertheless neutralized sufficiently to allow the concept to be repurposed in a new context. Their rewriting of Hjelmslev's terms is an explicit demonstration of this point – they retain his structure, but change his terms, so that 'matter' becomes 'body without organs', and so on.[11]

I tend to think Deleuze and Guattari's strategy is more productive because it forces a radical movement away from the problematic starting point. In this sense it is nearer to what might be termed Gramsci's strategy than Derrida's, if not in intent then certainly in effect. Imprisoned by the fascist government in Italy, Gramsci overcame censorship by inventing new words for old problematics and in the process reinvigorated Marxism, albeit at the price – according to Jameson – of a loss of connection with the radical tradition he was contributing to.[12] Censorship of the variety Gramsci faced was not something that Deleuze and Guattari had to contend with, obviously, but the problem they faced was equally tricky from a terminological perspective because they wanted to depart from, but not repudiate, both psychoanalysis and Marxism.

Although Deleuze and Guattari are often scathing in their remarks about Freud, they are nevertheless clear in saying they have no interest in throwing out psychoanalysis altogether; rather, they propose to re-engineer it. They are far more respectful in their comments on Marx, but they are equally clear in saying that there are certain aspects of Marxist theory, particularly the concept of ideology, that they wish to set aside.

Not only that, but they also wanted to short-circuit the connection between psychoanalysis and Marxism, so-called Freudo-Marxism, that emerged in the works of people like Fromm and Reich, whose work they admired. This made it difficult for them to continue using psychoanalytic and Marxist terminology without seeming to contradict themselves. By the same token, they wanted to anchor their own work in several of the key problematics underpinning both Freud's and Marx's work, so they couldn't use Derrida's strategy of writing terms under erasure without running the risk of cancelling out the very thing they wanted to preserve.

Gramsci's strategy was therefore better suited to what they were trying to do, even if it carried the risk of severing altogether the connections with the intellectual traditions they wanted to distance themselves from but not disavow. I think, though, that Jameson's concern that losing the word amounts to losing the problem is obviated by thinking of the movement between the two sets of terms as translation. I think of it as translation because as with all translations there is a quasi-equivalence between the term in the 'original' language and its rendering in the 'other' language, but that quasi-equivalence is to be found at the level of intent, as Benjamin suggests, rather than meaning. The underlying intent functions as a 'pure language' according to Benjamin that creates a sense of resonance between the two languages. In this context, intent should be understood in terms of the problem a given concept is animated by and ultimately answers to. In Deleuze and Guattari's case the problem which originated in an 'other' critical discourse persists in their concepts, but the solution does not, so new terms were required.

I doubt very much that in creating their new terms Deleuze and Guattari were greatly – if at all – influenced by Rudolf Pannwitz's judgement (cited approvingly by Benjamin in his essay on the task of the translator) as to what constitutes a good translation, but their work certainly embodies the spirit of what he suggests: 'The basic error of the translator is that he [*sic*] preserves the state in which his own language happens to be instead of allowing his language to be powerfully affected by the foreign tongue [. . .] He must expand and deepen his language by means of the foreign language.'[13] Much to the chagrin of many of their readers, Deleuze and Guattari's language is probably the most expanded and deepened language of any of the most significant philosophers of the twentieth century, with the possible exception of Derrida. Certainly, their work has been powerfully affected by the many different types of languages – clinical, autobiographical, poetic, philosophical, scientific, anthropological and so on – they embraced.

It needs to be underscored here that affected by clinical, autobiographical, poetic, philosophical, scientific and anthropological languages does not mean Deleuze and Guattari's conceptual language can be 'back translated' into the original language such that one can conclude they really were doing science (or whatever) after all. The languages remain distinct – they persist in their being – because translation hinges on the underlying problem, not the putative referent. If this is to be understood as 'influence' then it is best to grasp it in terms of what the new languages enable Deleuze and Guattari to think and say – they offer them a way of going beyond 'the taboos and constraints' they inherited from their own conceptual language.[14] But rather than dwell on the question of influence it is, I think, more useful to inquire about the different kinds of conversations their speaking in the tongues of clinical, autobiographical, poetic, philosophical scientific, and anthropological languages enables.

By avoiding the jargon of Marxism and to a lesser extent psychoanalysis Deleuze and Guattari opened up their work to a much broader audience than would otherwise have been the case. Their conceptually polysemic approach creates points of entry for a wide variety of disciplines that might not have been so interested had their language been of the drier philosophical variety or more overtly identified with Marxism and psychoanalysis. I tend to think Jameson is right though that one effect of dropping Marx's terms has been a generally de-marxified reading of their work, but one might also suppose that had they not done that they would have had far fewer readers for precisely that reason, namely the fact that critical theory as a whole is de-marxified.

This approach may seem to be at odds with Deleuze and Guattari's famous definition of philosophy as 'the art of forming, inventing, and fabricating concepts'.[15] Yet that is precisely what the translator must do: they have to invent a language that is in some sense adequate to the original, but also profoundly different, with new nuances that were impossible in the previous language. Of course, there are losses too, and in this sense Jameson's concern remains valid. But I think if we focus on the idea that the process of translation is one of confronting a problem and working through it to a solution it remains a useful way of overcoming the apparent intractability of Deleuze and Guattari's concepts. And Deleuze and Guattari are very clear on this point: 'All concepts are connected to problems without which they would have no meaning and which can themselves only be isolated or understood as their solution emerges.'[16]

Although they repeatedly insist that concepts have to be invented, they also insist that all concepts have a history, 'even though this history zigzags, though it passes, if need be, through other problems or onto different planes. In any concept there are usually bits or components that come from other concepts, which corresponded to other problems and presupposed other planes.'[17] This is because problems change and in changing they can connect or merge with other problems, and they can give rise to new problems as well. The point I'm trying to make is that if we start by trying to identify the problem that underpins any given concept in Deleuze and Guattari's arsenal and ask why they have translated it in the way they have then we're in a much better position to understand it than if we approach it from a natural language perspective or see it as an absolute novelty.

This book will be an extended demonstration of the viability of this claim. Needless to say, this way of tackling Deleuze and Guattari's thought should not be seen as an orthodoxy; rather, it is intended to function as a ladder that one kicks away when it is no longer required. There are three advantages, I believe, in seeing their conceptual inventions in this light. First, it negates the charge occasionally levelled at them of pursuing novelty for novelty's sake (the less polite version of the same charge is that their work is simply irrational). Second, it negates the common misunderstanding that their concepts can be understood as metaphors, or even more problematically as scientific or in some way veridical. Not even concepts like the nomad which appear to be derived from something factual can be treated as scientific or veridical. As Deleuze and Guattari themselves insist, it is the concept of the 'nomad' that explains nomadic behaviour, not the other way around.[18] The third advantage, which is in many ways the most important, is that the notion of translation saves us from the fallacy (I am tempted to say fantasy) that Deleuze and Guattari's concepts are invented *sui generis*, without any grounding in prior or ongoing 'discursive struggles' (to borrow Stuart Hall's useful notion).[19] This manifests in a number of ways, but the most common is what might be termed a 'naïve' reading which approaches Deleuze and Guattari's concepts from a natural language perspective.[20]

1 SCHIZOANALYSIS AND AFFECT

Even the history of philosophy is completely without interest if it does not undertake to awaken a dormant concept and to play it again on a new stage, even if this comes at the price of turning it against itself.[1]

When Deleuze first wrote about affect it was effectively a dormant concept (within his own philosophical milieu, at least) that he awakened and placed on a new stage. However, he accomplished it with such a deft sleight of hand no one noticed *his* contribution and mistook it for Spinoza's.[2] No one stopped to ask what problem Spinoza solves for Deleuze and Guattari. If one answers this question by saying Spinoza solves the problem of how to think about the body, which in a certain sense he does (although there is more to it than that), then one would still need to know what kind of a problem the body is and why it is a problem in Deleuze and Guattari's eyes. It is this second step that is missing from most – if not all – accounts of Deleuze and Guattari's encounter with Spinoza, as is evident in the work of such leading figures of affect theory and assemblage theory as Brian Massumi and Jane Bennett, both of whom presume Deleuze and Guattari are referring to actual, physical bodies when they speak about Spinoza's notion of affect.[3] That this is not the case is what we must come to understand if we are to grasp fully what Deleuze and Guattari mean by affect, and it becomes clear that it is not the case as soon as one inquires about the defining problem. As Deleuze and Guattari insist, 'concepts are only created as a function of problems which are thought to be badly understood or badly posed (pedagogy of the concept)'.[4] Affect is no exception to this rule. Deleuze and Guattari became interested in affect to the degree that the problem of human behaviour in the most general sense became the central focus of their work. As I argued in *Assemblage Theory and Method*, Deleuze and Guattari conceived of the concept of the assemblage as an intervention into behaviour studies. Affect must be viewed in the same light.

The Question of Schizoanalysis

This book continues the work begun in *Assemblage Theory and Method*, which is itself one part of a much larger project focused on schizoanalysis. Schizoanalysis, as I would want to define it, cannot be thought in the absence of either of the concepts of assemblage or affect, though many – including myself – have tried. Schizoanalysis is, as I have argued elsewhere, an incomplete project that Deleuze and Guattari worked on together and separately for more than thirty years. It remained incomplete at their deaths because the very scope of what they wanted to do was and remains beyond the capacity of two scholars, or indeed several. This is because the attempt to map history at the level as it unfolds of its unfolding will always be outpaced by history itself and that in a sense is what Deleuze and Guattari tried to do. For the same reason, we can continue their project today without either the pretence or conceit that we could somehow finish what they started.

Our way forward does not need to be conceived in linear terms, as though somehow we've been bequeathed a blueprint etched in stone and all we can do now is add an embellishment or two. I think, rather, that what we've inherited is a pile of rough workings-out that are like so many attempts – more or less successful – to design a machine capable of articulating the logic of life as it is lived today. Our job is to build test models of those designs and see if they work and, where necessary, correct the drawings. Getting Deleuze and Guattari 'right' means two things: first, it means grasping what it is they were trying to do and say in their own terms by asking what problem they were working on; second, it means asking whether or not their ideas actually work in relation to those problems. This, to me, is what a critical schizoanalysis would look like and it basically follows the pattern of Marxism and psychoanalysis, both of which are discursive fields that continue the incomplete projects of Marx and Freud.

Schizoanalysis is generally thought to be a form of anti-psychoanalysis, which in a way it is, but in practice this tends to result in a reading of their work that treats it as a kind of anti-analysis that, freed from the strictures of psychoanalysis (guilt, lack, the father and so on), refuses all obligations to say how things work and instead contents itself with applying labels to things (assemblage, rhizome, body without organs and so on). Accordingly, discussion of the conceptual foundations of schizoanalysis is perpetually postponed in favour of chanting the litany of the new freedoms Deleuze and Guattari's work has afforded us all by putting poor old Oedipus to the sword. However, this approach misses everything that is essential. Schizoanalysis is not simply, and certainly not only, a form of anti-psychoanalysis. Indeed, I would suggest that by focusing on their critique of psychoanalysis we cannot but miss what is essential in their work because that was not their starting point. As Deleuze says, philosophy always begins with a problem and we have the philosophy we deserve according to how well we define that problem. To the extent that Oedipus can be considered a problem such that they would write a book with the title *Anti-Oedipus*, we'd still need to ask why and under what conditions Oedipus *is* a problem.

As foundational as the problem of Oedipus is for their work, it is not the main objective of their project, which ultimately isn't about psychoanalysis at all. Deleuze makes this point explicit in an interview he gave several years after the publication of *Anti-Oedipus*: 'If our book was significant, coming after '68, it's because it broke with attempts at Freudo-Marxism: we weren't trying to articulate or reconcile different dimensions but trying to find a single basis for a production that was at once social and desiring in a logic of flows.'[5] The specific context of this remark is the refutation of the suggestion – which Deleuze says he finds 'shocking' – that his work with Guattari bears comparison with that of the so-called new philosophers. In doing so, he makes it clear that neither Oedipus nor psychoanalysis were ever the real targets of their critique: 'If Anti-Oedipus seeks to criticize psychoanalysis, it's in terms of a conception of the unconscious that, whether right or wrong, is set out in the book.'[6] He then goes onto note that by contrast the new philosophers simply denounce Marx and Marxism without presenting 'any new analysis of capital, which mysteriously drops out of consideration in their work'.[7] Later in the same interview he adds, 'what we need these days definitely isn't any critique of Marxism, but a modern theory of money as good as Marx's'.[8] This is needed, he says, because 'it's money that rules, money that communicates'.[9]

Although Deleuze does not use the term 'neoliberalism' here, which is perhaps surprising given that the interview took place in 1988 when the term was well and truly established in political circles, it is clear that this (in its incipient form, to be sure) is what he has in his sights. This is confirmed by his politically unfashionable Euroscepticism, which takes exception to the antidemocratic calls in the name of what would become the European Union to 'harmonize banking, insurance, internal markets, companies, police forces: consensus, consensus, consensus'.[10] But, he asks, 'what of people's becomings?'[11] Becomings, as Deleuze describes them here, are precisely what the state cannot control: 'May 68 was a *becoming* breaking through into history, and that's why history found it so hard to understand.'[12] Here then we see the actual problem that animates schizoanalysis: the relationship between people (figured in terms of their desire) and the social field (figured as a form of collective desire). The question that needs to be asked at this point, which I will try to answer in what follows, is: How does affect help us to develop and respond to *this* problem?

This problem is not unique to Deleuze and Guattari by any means; indeed, one could rightly say it is the central problematic of the entire field of critical theory. In the milieu Deleuze and Guattari were part of when they were writing together, Paris in the 1970s and 80s, the problem of social relations (in general) was typically approached from either a Marxist or a Freudian, or more usually a Marxist-Freudian, perspective. Deleuze and Guattari are no exception in this regard, but neither Marx nor Freud were a point of departure for them, and ultimately they rejected the accepted orthodoxies of both Marxism and Freudianism, without thereby rejecting either Marx or Freud. This is obviously a delicate path to tread and in the case of Freud in particular they often appear to be stepping outside of the line of productive engagement into rejecting his work *tout court*. But this is not the case and it is important to understand that both Freud and Marx are central to their project. If that is the case, though, one may wonder why they did not consider either Marx or Freud to be their point of departure. There are two answers to this question, both of which in quite different ways are pertinent to our inquiry.

To begin with, they were not interested in any kind of a return to the 'sacred texts of Freud and the sacred texts of Marx'.[13] They were especially uninterested in dealing with what they call the bureaucratic apparatuses that have sacralized the texts of Freud and Marx and by doing so strangled any and all experimentation. This is important because what they actually attempt to do with Marx and Freud is far bolder than the conjunctions proposed by the proponents of the Marxist-Freudian approach Deleuze and Guattari want to distinguish themselves from. In contrast to the

Marxist-Freudian approach, which seeks to reconcile the political economy with the libidinal economy, Deleuze and Guattari propose that there is only one economy: desiring-production: 'thus the problem of a genuine anti-psychiatric analysis is to show how unconscious desire sexually invests the forms of this economy as a whole'.[14] The key word here is 'invest' which, as I have explained elsewhere, is a codeword – or, if you prefer, a translation of a translation – for cathexis (itself a translation), which is the process in psychoanalysis whereby the libido as flow is converted into affect as discharge, or what Deleuze and Guattari call 'surplus value'.[15]

Why they should want to make this move, though, can only be understood by remembering that the problem that interested them was the relationship between people and the social field (i.e. social relations). This relationship, which in Deleuze and Guattari's time was variously theorized in terms of either domination or deception, stood in need of reconceptualization in their view because it could not account for the way desire seems always to escape its confines. In particular they were interested in people's enthusiasms, their revolutionary spirit, their susceptibility to being swept up by political movements that literally put them in the firing line.[16]

Guattari put it like this:

> We started with the idea that desire must not be conceived as a subjective superstructure that is more or less occluded. Desire never stops investing history, even in the darkest periods. The German masses had come to desire Nazism. After Wilhelm Reich, we cannot avoid coming to grips with this fact. Under certain conditions, the desire of the masses can turn against their own interests. What are those conditions? That is the question.[17]

Answering *that* question is the critical objective of schizoanalysis. Yet this has never been the focus of affect theory and assemblage theory, whose interests are elsewhere. One obvious reason why this objective has largely been neglected by these two fields is that it is essentially a Marxist question and both affect theory and assemblage theory have demonstrably turned away from the central tenets of Marxism. This is explicitly so in DeLanda's case. He says he is prevented from using Marx's concepts because he objects to Marx's labour theory of value and what he sees as an implicit teleology in the theory of the successive modes of production.[18] It runs deeper than that, though, because the fundamental premise of assemblage theory (particularly in its new materialist iterations) as it has evolved is contrary to Marx. As Jameson argued in a work that is a near contemporary of *Anti-Oedipus*, 'however materialistic such an approach to history [as one finds in the work of DeLanda, Bennett and those they have inspired] may seem, nothing is farther from Marxism than the stress on invention and technique as the primary cause of historical change'. Such theories, Jameson adds, 'function as a substitute for Marxist historiography in the way they offer a feeling of concreteness comparable to economic subject matter, at the same time that they dispense with any consideration of the human factors of classes and the social organisation of production'.[19]

In affect theory, the turning away from Marxism is less explicit, though still plain to see. No one could plausibly accuse Massumi, to take just one of affect theory's key figures, of being anti-Marx, yet the trajectory of his work is decidedly non-Marxist in its focus on people's interactions with objects, which he tends to theorize in terms of consumption rather than production. This is evident in his well-known discussion of the melting snowman experiment cited in the opening section of 'The Autonomy of Affect' which frames affect as being essentially a matter of a response to stimulus, or more pointedly a matter of contemplation.[20] This is in fact the opposite of the course taken by Marx.

Setting his sights on an earlier iteration of the approach taken by Massumi, Jameson delivers one of his most scathing indictments of contemporary philosophy. Its approach, he says, 'is ultimately socio-economic in character' and it is derived 'from the tendency of the middle classes to understand our relationship to external objects (and consequently our *knowledge* of those objects) in static and contemplative fashion. It is as though our primary relationship to things of the outside world were not one of making or use, but rather that of a motionless gaze, in a moment of time suspended, across a gap which it subsequently becomes impossible for thought to bridge'.[21] Contemporary philosophy's approach to objects reflects middle-class existence and its alienation from the real processes of production. The relationship of the middle classes to the objects they have, their commodities, the factories that produce them, and indeed the nature of capitalism itself, 'is a contemplative one, in that they are not aware of capitalism as a historical phenomenon, as being itself the result of historical forces [. . .] They can understand everything about their social environment (its elements, its functioning, its implicit laws) except the sheer historical existence of that environment itself'.[22]

Schizoanalysis, by contrast, by means of its archaeology of desire (e.g. the 'Savages, Barbarians, Civilized Men' chapter in *Anti-Oedipus*) confronts directly the question of the existence of the environment itself and in this regard offers a model of philosophy that is not grounded in contemplation, but is instead primarily concerned with production. Hence their well-known emphasis on the question: How does it work?

Cutting Out and Turning Over

Over the past two decades, affect theory and assemblage theory have evolved side by side, more or less independently of each other, with very little crossover between them, despite the fact that both movements acknowledge Deleuze and Guattari as a starting point.[23] This parting of the ways is not easily explained, but presumably it has to do with their differing objectives. It may be supposed, then, that assemblage theory did not give much attention to affect because it is primarily concerned with the interrelationships between material things, which can of course include bodies but does not extend to the vaporous 'intensities' often associated with affect. Likewise, it may be supposed that affect theory did not give much attention to the assemblage because it is primarily concerned with the interrelationships between bodies at the level of their vaporous 'intensities', which because of their intangible nature pose insurmountable conceptual difficulties for the different species of 'realist' philosophy that have taken an interest in the assemblage. As such, neither one needed the other, and for the most part never the twain did meet. Insofar as these two theoretical movements draw on the work of Deleuze and Guattari as their original source of inspiration, this can be regarded as two versions of the same misreading because they both fail to grasp one essential point: that for Deleuze and Guattari, there are no standalone concepts.

It is of course a deliberate provocation to call these two movements misreadings of Deleuze and Guattari's work, but as I acknowledged in *Assemblage Theory and Method*, I am quite prepared to see them as 'strong misreadings' in Harold Bloom's sense. But that does not mean, as I have tried to show with respect to the concept of the assemblage, that there isn't something important to be gained from returning to the source material with a view to avoiding making the same mistake twice. That 'something', I continue to believe, is a much richer analytic apparatus than either assemblage theory or affect theory offer on their own. Combining the two isn't as simple as adding them together, however, because the error they both make, in their own way, is to diverge from Deleuze and Guattari's original multidimensional conceptual model and perform the theoretical sleight of hand Michel de Certeau perceptively diagnosed as 'cutting out and turning over'. This two-step procedure takes place as follows: first, a concept (assemblage, affect) is *cut out* of its original context; second, the newly isolated concept is *turned over* so that it becomes the 'thing' that illuminates and sustains the whole enterprise, but still in a sense stands apart from it.[24] Here one thinks of the way both Manuel DeLanda and Jane Bennett separate the concept of the assemblage from desire and make it seem as though it is not first and foremost a matter of desire (as was explicit in the assemblage's conceptual precursor, the desiring-machine). They then turned the assemblage over and made it into the singular explanatory device capable of explaining everything that is generally perceived to be occurring today (the concept has attracted thousands of citations for precisely this reason).

I try to reverse this state of affairs, wherever I can, by (re)situating Deleuze and Guattari's concepts within the fabric of their work. But this is easier said than done because there is no obvious place to start. When Deleuze wrote in *Difference and Repetition* that deciding where to begin in philosophy is 'a very delicate problem' he may well have been speaking to his future readers about his own work because his style of writing, especially in his collaborations with Guattari, makes it difficult to know where to start.[25] There is no position, or concept, one can start with that is the foundation of all the others, so one is always compelled to start 'in the middle', as Deleuze puts it.[26] This is because, for Deleuze, 'concepts should express an event rather than an essence'.[27] All of Deleuze and Guattari's concepts are like this, they are all 'in the middle' of something – e.g. the assemblage sits in between the body without organs and the abstract machine, but at the same time it is the assemblage that 'makes' the body without organs and it is the assemblage that 'effectuates' the abstract machine. In other words, if one begins with the assemblage, one must also introduce both the body without organs and the abstract machine.

This is why *A Thousand Plateaus* is constructed as a series of 'split rings': you always need to circle back.[28] If, however, one takes the time to properly introduce all these concepts in detail at the outset before one even tries to say what affect is, then the specific character of affect risks being lost, and with it any interest in trying to figure out if affect is a useful concept. There is no easy solution to this problem, but I shall attempt to foreground affect in such a way that that it can be grasped in its specificity.

Bracketing Spinoza

In order to do that I need to present what I regard as an *enabling argument*, by which I mean it enables what I want to say in the book as a whole but does not pertain directly to what I want to say about affect. Putting it simply, though it is a far from simple point, it is my view that *Deleuze and Guattari create their own precursors* (as Borges famously said of Kafka). Deleuze and Guattari borrow freely and at times faithlessly from a wide variety of thinkers and writers but cannot be said to apply anyone's concepts but their own. While we can unpick the threads of their concepts, there is no value in trying to follow these threads back to points of origin, because to do so is to create the false impression that their work can – in the last instance – be conceived as either an application, or worse a derivation, of someone else's work. As Borges says of Kafka, their 'work modifies our conception of the past, as it will modify the future'.[29] To treat their work otherwise is to assume that they did not invent their own problems and contrive their own solutions, as they say every philosopher worth their salt should. As Deleuze and Guattari put it, 'those who do not renew the image of thought are not philosophers but functionaries who, enjoying a ready-made thought, are not even conscious of the problem and are unaware even of the efforts of those they claim to take as their models'.[30] In what follows then I show why it is wrongheaded to treat Deleuze and Guattari's work on affect as the straightforward continuation of Spinoza's work, as many in the field do. If, as I have suggested, the Spinoza who inspires Deleuze and Guattari is an invented precursor, then we have to examine the Spinoza they construct rather than the one we think they read.

As can be imagined, one of the most difficult aspects of writing this book has been figuring out the place Spinoza should be given in it. Over time, having blackened many pages with discarded false starts, I came to realize that the correct answer to that question is the opposite of what I, and I imagine everyone else, expected. I found that if I wanted to situate Spinoza in Deleuze and Guattari's project, particularly with regards to their development of the concept of affect, then I needed to *decentre Spinoza* in order to determine his proper place in the overall schema of their thought.[31] Decentre does not mean disregard, refute, much less negate, but it does mean carefully delimiting the extent to which Spinoza is treated as a philosophical resource by Deleuze and Guattari. This will no doubt strike many as misguided given how much Deleuze wrote about Spinoza (books, articles, lectures and so on). Regardless of how much Deleuze wrote about Spinoza, that does not mean it is accurate, much less useful, to think of his work as Spinozist.

As a conceptual artisan Deleuze found new ways of formulating concepts in Spinoza, which he then used these to formulate his *own* concepts. There are no off-the-shelf concepts in Deleuze and Guattari's work. Affect is no exception to this rule. In *What is philosophy?* Deleuze and Guattari insist that every concept bears the signature of its creator and that as a consequence no two iterations of a concept are the same, not even when they appear to be the same as is the case with affect, which has had several different creators over the centuries. Deleuze and Guattari acknowledge that each new iteration of a concept inevitably incorporates elements of its previous iterations, but this does not mean that taken together they form a diachronic lineage such that the latest iteration can be regarded as a development and extension of the first iteration.

Obviously enough, Deleuze and Guattari are not the first philosophers to make use of the concept of affect, and certainly their version bears traces of previous versions of the concept, including Spinoza's version, but we can nevertheless insist – following the logic of Deleuze and Guattari's own account of the relation between different uptakes of a concept – that their version of affect is uniquely their own. It may be, and indeed I would suggest that it is, the case that their version of affect is a synthesis of several different theoretical sources, both philosophical and scientific (Spinoza and Uexküll among others). This means in dealing with Deleuze and Guattari's work we can and should *bracket* – in the phenomenological sense – all other versions of affect besides their own and thereby suspend any 'common sense' assumptions we might want to make about the connections between them. This includes both those authors we want to claim as Deleuze and Guattari's source material – Spinoza, Nietzsche, Hume and so on – and those authors like Lauren Berlant, Eve Kosofsky Sedwick, Elspeth Probyn and Greg Seigworth (among many others), who – to a greater or lesser extent – claim Deleuze and Guattari as their source material.

All the bracketed iterations of affect should be regarded as existing in the state Deleuze and Guattari refer to, following Rémy Chauvin, as *aparallel evolution*.[32] Each version evolves on its own according to its own set of problems and while there may be a transfer of 'genetic material' between the various iterations, no one version can be considered causal in relation to any other. This 'transfer' should not be confused with a process of evolution, whereby a concept maintains its basic identity as it passes from one philosopher to another. Deleuze was clear about this: his concepts are bastard children and monsters.

This applies particularly to Spinoza's concept of affect, which is all too often treated as though it is a necessary precursor to Deleuze and Guattari's concept of affect. Indeed, it would not be an exaggeration to say that it is generally thought that Deleuze and Guattari's use of the term 'affect' derives solely from Deleuze's account of Spinoza. But this is simply a mistake which reflects, I assume, a failure to grasp Deleuze and Guattari's work 'as a whole', as they insist one should with any philosopher. Not only that, insofar as we persist in thinking that Deleuze and Guattari's use of the term 'affect' derives solely from Deleuze's account of Spinoza we fail to see both the originality of Deleuze and Guattari's conception of affect and its structural importance to their development of schizoanalysis as a critical methodology. To which I would add, it is only in the light of the latter – the development of schizoanalysis as a critical methodology – that one can actually grasp what they mean by affect. Spinoza is important to their project, as are a range of other philosophical and non-philosophical authors, as I will discuss in a moment, so we need to be careful not to make it seem as though schizoanalysis is in some way derived from Spinoza when (at most) it merely incorporates elements of his work. We need to stop treating affect as a ready-made concept Deleuze and Guattari simply picked out of a catalogue and inserted into their own work and instead treat it as something they invented for themselves.

It is of course beyond question that Spinoza's work informs the schizoanalytic project, but we need to be careful not to exaggerate its importance. We should not be tempted into thinking that when Deleuze and Guattari say in *Anti-Oedipus* that it was Spinoza who saw clearly 'the fundamental problem of political philosophy', namely the strange fact that people appear to fight for their own servitude, that this means they are 'using' Spinoza after all, because the answer they give is not Spinozist.[33]

As tempting as it may be to think that one can settle questions about the nature of Deleuze and Guattari's concepts simply by consulting the apparent originating author, in this case Spinoza, it is a false trail. This should really be obvious enough to go without saying because there is necessarily a distinction to be made between Spinoza's thought and Deleuze's account of Spinoza's thought in the lectures, books and essays he devoted to Spinoza, and yet another distinction between Deleuze's exegetical early work and his later work, especially his collaboration with Guattari, in which he sought to do philosophy 'for himself'. Yet it is an easy mistake to make because the (often) obscure nature of the later books can lead one to assume, out of desperation perhaps, that the earlier books must contain a clue to their meaning. However, this forgets that these works had very different purposes. The former were written in a consciously exegetical fashion (e.g. the books on Bergson and Kant were written for an 'introductory' monograph series), albeit creatively so, while the latter pursued a highly inventive path. As such, it follows that there is a distinction to be made between Spinoza's concept of affect and Deleuze and Guattari's concept of affect.

It is true that Deleuze often claims an underground affinity between the disparate works he draws inspiration from, as though to say they too have Spinoza in them, as he does with Beckett, Hjelmslev, T. E. Lawrence and Uexküll. He even goes so far as to claim that Nietzsche, D. H. Lawrence, Kafka and Artaud should be considered disciples of Spinoza.[34] In *What is Philosophy?* Deleuze and Guattari say that there is 'such force in those unhinged works of Hölderlin, Kleist, Rimbaud, Michaux, Pessoa, Artaud, and many other English and American novelists, from Melville to Lawrence or Miller, in which the reader discovers admiringly that they have written the novel of Spinozism'.[35] In every case, though, the Spinozism exhibited by these diverse authors is of the order of a 'a philosophically bearded Hegel [and] a philosophically clean-shaven Marx', that is to say they are doubles achieved by virtue of 'maximal modification', which is precisely why Deleuze admires them.[36] He even admits that his own approach to the philosophical works of figures he admires follows the logic of a certain Pierre Menard who in Borges's tale set out to write *Don Quixote* from scratch not by imitating Cervantes, but by being himself, such that the copy is 'truer' than the original.[37] Deleuze's books and essays on Spinoza provide a framework and launching pad for his collaborative work with Guattari and in this respect it is helpful to revisit them, providing it is borne in mind that the Spinoza who appears in their work is the Spinoza they have conjured in order to develop answers to their own questions.

Bracketing Spinoza's concept of affect within Deleuze and Guattari's work helps us to see the originality of their conception of affect by allowing us to acknowledge that it exists and that it is an important resource, and at the same time resist the temptation to treat it as an essential (or even *the*) progenitor of Deleuze and Guattari's concept of affect. It means we can acknowledge that in fact several different conceptions of affect are cited across the span of Deleuze and Guattari's collaboration and not have to wonder how we're going to reconcile the differences between them (e.g. Uexküll's concept of affect as a simple capacity, in a tick for example, is not the same as Spinoza's concept of affect, which has a moral dimension, despite the fact Deleuze and Guattari constantly draw parallels between them, because their corresponding relations to action are different – the tick is portrayed as purely passive, only ever responding to external triggers, with no capacity for becoming active). Similarly, it means we can acknowledge the existence of a variety of different versions of the concept of affect (and there are many as even the most cursory Google search reveals) without needing to either try to incorporate them into our understanding of Deleuze and Guattari's version and somehow claim a hitherto unnoticed compatibility exists or negate them.

Manifestly in the Air

As Deleuze once said of the concept of difference, the subject dealt with here is manifestly in the air, but affect theory is very far from being a coherent field.[38] It is not my intention here to try to resolve all of the difficulties current in affect theory today; my rather more modest goal is to try to disentangle the specific nature of Deleuze and Guattari's contribution to this topic. As will be seen in what follows, disentangling Deleuze and Guattari's contribution to affect theory ultimately means showing that affect theory has never really been Deleuzian in any meaningful sense, despite appearances and declarations to the contrary.

Insofar as the critical humanities are concerned, affect theory is drawn from two main sources, Silvan Tompkins and Gilles Deleuze, with Eve Kosofsky Sedgwick as the champion of the former and Brian Massumi the champion of latter (despite the fact that Deleuze plays a relatively small role in his elaboration of affect). I do not think it would be an injustice to add here that Massumi's intent in pioneering essays like 'The

Autonomy of Affect', which many regard as a founding text for affect theory, was to fashion his own theory of affect, rather than explicate Deleuze's. Certainly, Deleuze features very little in that essay. Both the Tomkins-Sedgwick and Deleuze-Massumi schools of affect theory (as they might usefully be known) have been very productive, sparking thousands of academic articles in the past three decades. With very few exceptions, this work has largely been accepted at face value, perhaps because of its apparent scientificity. As several critics have pointed out, both schools always present affect as that which has somehow escaped notice before now and is 'missing' from critical analyses in the humanities. The implication is that by 'failing' to account for affect humanities scholars aren't grasping what is really going on in contemporary culture.[39] Affect has effectively become a new kind of truth, replacing ideology and semiology, by postulating the existence of a 'deeper' non-discursive truth these fields of inquiry cannot reach.

In the limited instances where affect theory has been subject to critical interrogation the evaluation of the connection to Deleuze is usually placed in the 'too hard' basket, presumably with the idea that such matters are best left to 'professional' Deleuze scholars. In *The Ascent of Affect*, Ruth Leys's comprehensive critical survey of contemporary work on the notion of affect, a single, but I think revealing, footnote is dedicated to the work of Deleuze (indicatively, she ignores Guattari). Noting that Deleuze is probably 'the most influential figure in the rise of the new affect theory', she says, 'it is invariably an open question as to the accuracy with which one or another affect theory represents his views'.[40] She then says, somewhat surprisingly given the unrelentingly critical tone of the whole book, that she will leave it to others to answer that question. It is a surprising move on her part because it is clear from her comments elsewhere in the book that she thinks the answer to that question is obvious, namely that affect theory does not give an accurate account of Deleuze's thought. In a chapter that takes to task noted Deleuze and Guattari scholars Brian Massumi and John Protevi for their overreliance on and – in her eyes – misreading of cognitive psychology, Leys writes, 'it is striking how compatible Deleuze-inspired definitions of affect as a nonlinguistic, bodily "intensity" turn out to be with the Tomkins-Ekman paradigm'.[41] The undertone of suspicion here is unmistakable and I think justified. The overemphasis on the inarticulate and the bodily Leys detects is, I would suggest, a function of this double-sided misrepresentation of their thought as philosopher-psychologists, a conjunction which despite the best efforts of Antonio Damasio to popularize should be resisted in the case of Deleuze and Guattari. Short-circuiting this all-too-easy reliance on experimental psychology should be seen as a necessary 'negative task' of schizoanalysis.

In spite of the influence Deleuze and Guattari's work has had on the field of affect theory, particularly in cultural studies (broadly defined), it has not been well-served by its proponents who, when not making them sound like psychologists rather than philosophers, treat them as latter-day Spinozists who apply ready-made concepts instead of the inventors they actually were. Yet it seems no one is willing to take up the duty of performing the 'negative task' of combating misrepresentations of their thought. In Papoulias and Callard's important survey of affect theory 'Biology's Gift', a single footnote is again all that is dedicated to Deleuze (Guattari is again ignored) and similarly it's quite telling, and not only because despite noting the importance of Deleuze's thought to affect theory it also declines to interrogate the readings of his work the field has generated. They write, '[T]he turn to affect is associated with several other theoretical and substantive preoccupations: these include investigations of vitalism; engagements with technoscience (and an increased focus on "information" as opposed to signification); and reconceptualizations of organic and non-organic (and the human-animal) distinction. A genealogy of this shift in preoccupations and theoretical touchstones would certainly need to narrate and assess the role that the assimilation of (certain aspects of) Gilles Deleuze's thought into theory.'[42] The key phrase here, buried in parenthesis, is the observation that only certain aspects of Deleuze's thought appear to have been significant to the development of affect theory. One could probably narrow it down even further and limit it to just a handful of pages that have been cited, most of them ripped from a single chapter of Deleuze's work on Spinoza.

That a sound genealogy of affect theory would need to assess the uptake of Deleuze's thought is amply confirmed by the two collections, which have served as touchstones for the emerging field for more than a decade as the many thousands of citations they have each garnered can attest: *The Affective Turn: Theorizing the Social* (2007) and *The Affect Theory Reader* (2010), edited by Patricia Ticineto Clough, and Melissa Gregg and Greg Seigworth, respectively. Both collections feature Deleuze as well as Deleuze and Guattari extensively: in the case of Clough, the earlier of the two volumes, Tomkins is a relatively minor player, which is striking given how dominant in the field his work would later become;

while for Gregg and Seigworth, Tomkins and Deleuze are presented as equals, and framed as elective affinities rather than critical choices.[43] On this point, my impression is that Hemmings is not wrong in saying that it is a preference for 'Tomkins's pragmatism or Deleuze's imaginative flights' that carries the day rather than the specific ontological and epistemological differences that actually separate them.[44] While it is true that the Deleuze and Guattari found in these pages is not always directly tied to Spinoza, the connection to his work simmers beneath the surface like an underground magma flow, to borrow an image from Deleuze, making its presence felt in the treatment of their work as essentially a philosophy of the body. Probyn's chapter on shame in the Gregg and Seigworth volume is emblematic in this regard inasmuch that her discussion of Deleuze, which otherwise has nothing to do with Spinoza, but focuses instead on T. E. Lawrence and Primo Levi, albeit through a Deleuzian lens, nevertheless grounds itself in Deleuze's account of affect in Spinoza's philosophy of the body.[45]

Any sound genealogy of affect theory would also reveal the fact that, as influential as Deleuze has been in shaping the field, Massumi's work has been far more influential. 'The problem,' Massumi says, 'is that there is no cultural-theoretical vocabulary specific to affect.'[46] Despite his lament, Massumi's definition of affect as an asignifying intensity would make any such vocabulary impossible because as he specifies affect and intensity are 'akin to what is called a critical point, or a bifurcation point, or singular point, in chaos theory and the theory of dissipative structures'.[47] As he goes onto clarify, the critical point 'is the turning point at which a physical system paradoxically embodies multiple and normally mutually exclusive potentials, only one of which is selected [. . .] The organization of multiple levels that have different logics and temporal organizations, but are locked in resonance with each other and recapitulate the same event in divergent ways, recalls the fractal ontology and nonlinear causality underlying theories of complexity'.[48] The paradox of Massumi's definition of affect is that for all his talk about 'real emergence' it has neither substance nor form: it is pure process.[49] The emphasis here on the multiple levels of affect acting simultaneously is crucial and it is something I will come back to under the general rubric of the problem of the composition of affect.

Naming and classifying particular species of affect is impossible in Massumi's terms, yet that is precisely what Deleuze and Guattari set out to do with their concepts of the body without organs, the abstract machine and the assemblage. Massumi positions Spinoza as a starting point for the development of his concept of affect. He writes, Spinoza 'talks of the body in terms of its capacity for affecting or being affected [...] When you affect something, you are at the same time opening yourself to being affected in turn, and in a slightly different way than you might have been the moment before. You have made a transition [...] Affect is this passing of a threshold, seen from the point of view of the change in capacity'.[50] Massumi calls the feeling associated with this transition 'thinking-feeling' because 'it is imbued with an immediate understanding of what is under way, what might be coming – and what we are becoming'.[51] As such, it is an *enactive* understanding, he says, that is at one with the action. He goes on to clarify that this thinking-feeling is not the thinking or feeling of either an object or subject but pertains rather to an event: it is that which passes between the object and subject, and should therefore be considered pre-subjective, which is to say it can only be retrospectively 'owned' by the subject.[52] This last point, however, would seem to contradict the previous point that affect is imbued with an understanding of what the subject is becoming and suggest that far from being pre-subjective it is in fact better understood as intra-subjective, i.e. a transformational movement internal to a subject. But that is not the direction Massumi takes.

Instead, he says that affect is *transindividual*, which he defines as a form of '*differential attunement* between two bodies in a joint activity of becoming'.[53] He means 'that the bodies in [an] encounter are both completely absorbed in the felt transition, but they are differently absorbed, coming at it asymmetrically, from different angles [...] But all of these differences are actively, dynamically co-implicated in the event, as immediate dimensions of the event, the *same* unfolding event'.[54] There are two key points here that shape Massumi's conception of affect, neither of which are consistent with Spinoza or Deleuze even though both are attributed to them. First, affect is constantly characterized as an interaction between two bodies more or less colliding into one another, and not as something that can be generated from within. This is extremely limiting, to say the least, and it effectively makes impossible Deleuze and Guattari's notion of becoming, which may occur in relation to another object or subject but is not necessarily triggered by that relation or encounter. Second, Massumi emphasizes that the transition which occurs in an affective encounter is real and actual, which again is not the case with Deleuze and Guattari's concept of becoming. The Wolf-Man's becoming-animal is real, but not actual: he does not become a wolf, nor does he necessarily think that is what is happening to him.

For Massumi, the notion of an unwilled 'change in capacity' is what is essential here because it enables him to theorize affect as a 'margin of manoeuvrability' which coincides with every action and in that sense has the appearance and function of hope.[55] It basically means that no matter what happens in the course of one's life things could always be, or have been, different, providing one can find the means of effecting what he calls a 'phase shift' in the frequency of one's affects. The problem here is that nothing in Massumi's account of affect actually licenses this way of characterizing it as what I would call a quasi-moral category (it assumes that hope is unequivocally 'good', even 'virtuous', which is surely debatable as critics of Obama's emphasis on hope in his election campaigns made apparent – hope is what we have when progressive change is unlikely). On the contrary, Massumi takes great pains to push all thinking about affect in completely the opposite direction, ultimately (in his later work) towards the non-philosophical realms of cognitive science. 'It's important to remember,' he says, 'that Spinoza uses this to talk about the body [. . .] A body is defined by what capacities it carries from step to step [. . .] A body's ability to affect or be affected – its charge of affect – isn't something fixed.'[56] But hope is not a purely bodily capacity – it may be a qualification of a bodily capacity, but it is not bodily in itself.

To characterize affect in this way is to overcode it and endow it with a significance that is at odds with the actual definition Massumi gives because by his own account affect is an asignifying, contentless, pure galvanic response to stimulus, an intensity and not an extensive content-filled emotion like hope. Moreover, it glosses over the fact that different is not necessarily better; things can always be worse than they are, which would suggest that characterizing affect as hope puts it in the same class of categories as the imagination and indeed fantasy. Massumi acknowledges that there is 'nothing essentially liberatory or progressive about affect', yet the entire trajectory of his account of it contradicts this statement. And it leads him to make some philosophically and politically problematic claims that not only undercut the coherence of the concept, but also undermine its critical potential. For instance, he says, the 'concept of affect I find useful is Spinoza's well-known definition. Very simply, he says that affect is "the capacity to affect or be affected".'[57] He expands upon this by stating that it is a relational definition 'because it places affect in the space of relation: between an affecting and a being affected'. Somewhat strangely he says this means it 'forbids separating passivity from activity', which is effectively the opposite of what both Deleuze and Spinoza say.[58] Indeed, central to their accounts is the fact that affecting is active while being affected is necessarily passive, which in turn raises the question of how and whether the latter can ever be converted into the former. If we could not distinguish between affecting and being affected then we would lose the possibility of attributing causality and just as importantly apportioning culpability.

It would mean we could not distinguish between assailant (affecter) and victim (affected), or worse it would mean that we would have to conclude that the assailant was affected by their victim, and that this somehow contributed to their actions. Matters are not helped in this regard by conceiving of affect as a *power of resistance*. Massumi proposes that because Spinoza defines the state of being affected as a capacity, which means it can be thought of as an action in its own right. This, presumably, is how he arrives at the idea that passive and active cannot be separated in the case of affect. If so, it is false reasoning because an action is not automatically active, indeed the whole point of the distinction between active and passive is to distinguish between those actions that are really just reactions because we are not the true cause of the action. For instance, if someone insults me and I get mad, my actions are reactions because I'm not the true cause of the action. My action would not have occurred if I had not been provoked, so it does not qualify as active. Even if we put this point aside, Massumi's attempt to define resistance as action is still problematic because it runs aground on the same problem of the misattribution of causality indicated above.

Massumi writes:

The force of a blow, for example, is a product of an impinging force *meeting* a force of resistance, a certain capacity to resist. That capacity is a mode of activity of the body. It is a doing, as much as the blow itself (it is the body asserting its structural integrity, bracing itself in a certain manner to absorb, deflect, dodge the blow, or even, as in martial arts, to turn its force back against the author).[59]

All of these actions – absorbing, deflecting, dodging and so on – are reactions to an action they did not initiate and for this reason remain passive regardless of the fact that in a purely physical sense they constitute actions of the body. But this does not mean the initiating action that prompted these reactions was any less passive – someone throwing a punch is not necessarily active in their actions because, as I said, it may be that the blow was issued as a reaction to something someone said or did. Moreover, a dodged blow is still a wrong and the dodger still wronged because of the intent behind it, so it is important to retain the distinction between acting and acted upon.

The real problem here, though, as I alluded to above, is the assumption that affect is solely an affair of the body, when in reality affects can be generated from within by the mind. This emphasis on the bodily more than any other single factor limits the way affect theory can be mobilized in the service of understanding everyday life because the majority of affects are not bodily. For instance, if I like a piece of music because of the memories it evokes, this is still a matter of affect and affects but it operates on several registers at once, not just the bodily. Indeed, as Oliver Sacks reports, it is perfectly possible to hear music in one's mind without any external stimulus at all; the sound and the associated affect are produced purely neurologically. Apparently, too, the commonest cause of this type of hallucination is the onset of deafness.[60] To focus solely on the bodily aspect of listening to music limits what affect as a concept can help us to explain. Another reason why affect needs to be reconnected with the assemblage.

The limited nature of the exclusively bodily version of affect can be seen very clearly in Massumi. He positions affect as that which cultural studies misses because it is too concerned with texts and their meanings. That Deleuze and Guattari treat signs as affects seems to be forgotten in the haste to present affect as something radically new and somehow missing from cultural studies. In affect theory, then, the meaninglessness of the visceral is thus valorized over the meaningfulness of the textual, with the former treated as a kind of 'truth' that the latter conceals. The misprision at the heart of affect theory is this: just because a body may be defined in terms of its affects, i.e. its capacity to be affected and to affect others, that does not also mean that only bodies are capable of affects, much less that affects are essentially bodily. I am tempted to suggest that affect theory has found itself in this position because it has only ever looked to Deleuze and Guattari as a bag of tricks, or more generously a toolbox, from which concepts can be borrowed at will, and not as a body of work that needs to be engaged with 'as a whole' in order to properly grasp its logic. Affect theory, as it has evolved over the last two decades, seems only to acknowledge the existence of bodily affects and not the full range of bodily and non-bodily affects that one finds in both Spinoza's work and Deleuze's account of it. As such, there is an obvious need to ask the question: What did Deleuze and Guattari actually mean by affect and how does this concept fit into the overall schema of their schizoanalytic project?

2 OVERWHELMED BY DESIRE

The history of philosophy, rather than repeating what a philosopher says, has to say what he [sic] must have taken for granted.[1]

Meeting Life

The argument I am presenting here, takes seriously what one might call an everyday understanding of affect, i.e. the understanding of affect one finds in 'pop' psychology books of the 'self-help' variety (e.g. Carlos Castenada's series of books, about which Deleuze and Guattari say the fact that they are probably fake only makes them more interesting) and in everyday settings (itself a reflection of the pervasive influence of 'pop' psychology and the many iterations of psychotherapy people practise under the auspices of 'self-care') as a means of understanding and explaining certain types of behaviours.[2] I do not intend to survey this literature, which would take us well beyond the scope of what I am trying to do here, and is too vast and varied for a meaningful summation in any case, but I do want to briefly touch on what I take to be one of the central tenets of its approach to affect because in a very general way it is consistent with the one I want to develop here inasmuch as it treats affect as the capacity to 'meet life' (I'll explain the origin of this phrase in a moment). Consistent with 'pop' psychology does not mean identical to 'pop' psychology. There are important differences between Deleuze and Guattari's approach to affect and the approach taken by 'pop' psychology. For Deleuze and Guattari, affect is neither instinctual nor personal, as it tends to be regarded in several branches of contemporary psychology, but rather productive and machinic, or as I prefer to put it, capacitating. But insofar as there is always a therapeutic dimension to what they write, 'pop' psychology can help sensitize us to a way of reading Deleuze and

Guattari's work that does not simply recite truisms about their debt to Spinoza, but instead seeks to understand their project in its own terms. By therapeutic I do not mean clinical, or psychological, I mean simply a concern for identifying the ways and means by which we can live more fulfilling lives. This comes through in the many cautions Deleuze and Guattari issue – do not destratify too fast, do not deterritorialize too far, do not generate cancerous bodies without organs, and so on.

If this approach seems strange, or worse invalid, because it seems to want to draw too close to 'unreliable' sources then perhaps it will help to recall that the majority of 'cases' Deleuze and Guattari present in support of their hypotheses, and from which they derive their concepts, are drawn from non-technical sources, such as autobiographies, biographies, literary works of all types (poems, plays, novels, short stories and so on), art, opera, self-help books and so on. Deleuze and Guattari literally draw on all kinds of texts (plant biology, ethology, quantum physics, metallurgy and so on) to construct their 'map' of the 'mind', very few of which are directly related to psychology or the neuro sciences. 'For literature is like schizophrenia: a process and not a goal, a production and not an expression.'[3] In *What is Philosophy?* they describe non-philosophical works as a vital resource that philosophy cannot do without. '*Philosophy needs a non-philosophy that comprehends it; it needs a non-philosophical comprehension just as art needs non-art and science needs non-science.*'[4]

'Pop' psychology, along with all the other non-philosophical sources Deleuze and Guattari draw on, functions as a kind of yardstick by which we can measure the success or failure, which is to say the efficacy, of the concepts Deleuze and Guattari invent. It is not a matter of swapping one for the other, but of reading them together and allowing one to 'translate' the other (in Benjamin's sense) until we see both words differently. Deleuze and Guattari do not treat non-philosophical sources as either factual or veridical in an empirical sense, but they nevertheless ascribe to them a diagnostic value implying that they regard such works as articulating a kind of 'truth' about specific types of psychosocial formations (i.e. assemblages) and their relation to mental functioning (i.e. affect). Writers, Deleuze says, are physicians of themselves and of the world. 'The world is a set of symptoms whose illness merges with man [*sic*]. Literature then appears as an enterprise of health', or, as I would prefer to put it, a therapeutics.[5]

In 'pop' psychology affect is what enables us to get out of bed in the morning, to go for a run, write a book, fall in love, and so on. It is not what we feel at a given moment, but rather the capacity to feel anything at all. It is the baseline for all of our emotional responses – it isn't a matter of being happy or sad, but rather of being capable of being happy or sad, where to feel sad is considerably better than feeling nothing at all. Affect is what enables us to interact with the world, to feel good about ourselves and others, to want to pat dogs, to listen to music, to dance, and to start a revolution. It finds expression in mood, feelings and emotions, but always operates on a different level. A good mood is an expression of an upbeat affect – our mood may be spoilt by a tasteless remark, or the weather becoming inclement and ruining a pleasant walk in the park, but this change in our mood does not necessarily stem from or register at the level of our affect. Even if we felt our walk was spoiled by the rain we may continue to think of ourselves as happy.

Affect in this sense is our capacity to be in a good mood, irrespective of what is happening around us. Someone who is seemingly incapable of being in a good mood is usually described as lacking in affect, or perhaps suffering from flattened affect. For instance, Alice James suffered from what her mother described as a 'feeling of inability to meet life'.[6] If, like Henry and William James's sister, someone appears to lack the capacity to remain in an 'up' or good mood, or else bounce back after being in a low or bad mood, then their affect is said to lack tolerance. People classified as, or identifying as, neurodivergent are said to have a 'different' affect, which capacitates them in ways neurotypical people may find difficult to appreciate or comprehend.

Although it is a relatively trivial example, thinking about how we feel about sunshine on any given day is a useful way to begin to unpack at least some of the complexities of affect. If we were to ask why our capacity to be happy responds positively to this thing – sunshine – and negatively to some other thing – rain – then we would be forced to suppose at least two things: first, that the composition of affect differs between people, or otherwise we would all respond in the same way to the same stimuli; second, that affect functions selectively, it does not respond equally appreciatively to all stimuli, but neither does it respond in the same way every time. This, in turn, presents us with a third possible supposition, that the composition of affect is the key to understanding Deleuze and Guattari's way of thinking about affect.

On a cold day, rain is usually experienced as miserable and annoying, but on a hot day it might come as a cool relief. How we feel in these situations depends on our affect as the capacity to feel and relate. The fact that we experience the same stimuli differently, both as individuals and collectively, i.e. some of us like sunshine some of the time, but perhaps not all the time, and not necessarily at the same time as others, means that we cannot treat affect like a machine that has only one setting – we need to account for its variability. But that is easier said than done. If the same stimuli produce different responses in different people, or even in the same person at different times, then the variability of affect cannot be explained solely in terms of stimulus and response. It is not different sunshine that explains the differences in people's responses to the feeling of sun on their face; rather it is *differently perceived* sunshine that explains the differences in their responses. This also rules out the idea that affect is exclusively, much less ultimately, bodily because as this example shows, affect is a matter of how we feel *about* the feeling of something.

Affect is not something we feel in response to a given situation, it is the foundation and limit of what we are *able to feel* in response to a given situation. This should not be taken to mean either that our affect is unchanging or that it cannot be altered by certain types of experiences. Our affect requires constant nurturing to sustain its capacity to meet the day. This is the essential work performed by assemblages. Music offers a clear illustration of this point. Deleuze and Guattari regard it as *so* affecting, i.e. affect altering, that they ascribe to it a fascist potential: 'music (drums, trumpets) draws people and armies into a race that can go all the way to the abyss (much more so than banners and flags, which are paintings, means of classification and rallying)'.[7] Here affecting should be understood as inducing a variation in the constitution of affect as a capacity to feel rather than a specific type of feeling. It is not the same thing as a response to a stimulus because it refers to a change in one's capacity to meet the day. These two points are not mutually exclusive, of course, but it is important nonetheless to distinguish between them, or else the latter will simply collapse into the former and affect will be reduced to a response. Affect is in this sense involuntary – it would perhaps be more accurate to describe it as what we cannot help but feel.

The capacity to meet life is unbidden, either we have it or we don't. Doubtless this is part of the appeal of mood-altering intoxicants and 'thrill-seeking' behaviour: it seems to possess the capacity to change what we otherwise experience as helplessness in the face of our own capacity to meet life. It is noteworthy in this regard that Deleuze and Guattari describe drug use as an unsustainable means of enhancing our capacity to meet life. By the same token, one can certainly understand Spinoza's point when he says the mind constantly 'strives to imagine those things that increase or aid the body's power of acting', but this presumes the existence of an agency that determines our capacity to act which the mind seeks to fuel.[8] That agency is affect.

Deleuze and Guattari's brief comments on drugs are instructive for our purposes here because they conceive of the drug experience as a transformation of affect which manifests as a change in the capacity to perceive the world. For Deleuze and Guattari the philosophical interest of psychoactive drugs, whose use outside of a clinical setting they ultimately reject as unsustainable and dangerous, is the mark they have left on non-users. 'If the experimentation with drugs has left its mark on everyone, even non-users, it is because it changed the perceptive coordinates of space-time and introduced us to a universe of microperceptions in which becomings-molecular take over where becomings-animal leave off.'[9] Drugs make apparent something that is central to all forms of becoming: it manifests as a change in perception – not only in terms of *what* is seen, but also in terms of *how* things are seen.

The drug experience, as Deleuze and Guattari describe it (borrowing from Michaux's account of his experiences with mescaline), is not dissimilar to Lovecraft's account of Carter's nightmare: 'Nothing left but the world of speeds and slownesses without form, without subject, without face. Nothing left but the zigzag of a line, like the "lash of the whip of an enraged cart driver" shredding faces and landscapes.'[10] As such drugs can be considered an agent of becoming, according to Deleuze and Guattari, but it is always overlaid 'by hallucinations, delusions, false perceptions, phantasies, or paranoid outbursts'.[11] Hence their interest in Henry Miller's notion of getting drunk on pure water – it offers a form of self-transformation that can be induced by the self without the risk of toxic drugs.[12]

Desire is Overwhelming

Deleuze and Guattari's work is usually taken to be a celebration of desire, but in many ways their central message is that desire is overwhelming, indeed it is so overwhelming at times that we need to retreat to what they call the body without organs. The idea that we suffer from the demands of our own desires is central to psychoanalysis too, of course, where it is usually coded in terms of the fear of self-reproach. We feel guilty for desiring what we know or feel we shouldn't desire. It is the guilt that we suffer from, not the desire itself. This model assumes two things: first, that if we did not internalize societal demands we would not suffer from our desires, we would simply live according to our instincts; second, that it is precisely because of our internalization of societal demands in the form of taboos that we are prevented from living purely brutish lives. There are two such demands which are generally considered 'universal' by psychoanalysis: the taboos against homicide and incest, which in combination form the basis of Freud's notion of the Oedipal complex. Freud will go so far as to make the guilt we feel in the face of forbidden desires the organizational principle of our unconscious, such that all our thoughts and feelings can be traced back to these two taboos which he finds perfectly expressed in Sophocles. According to this model, we are the subjects we are because we repress, sublimate or delay certain of our instincts, which given free rein might lead us to contravene these taboos. Delayed gratification is synonymous with civilized life in Freud. The instinctual demands we delay do not disappear altogether, so we feel their pressure even though we have 'managed' them in some way (repression, sublimation, delay), and that causes us to feel self-reproach. We feel guilty for having the thought we could not fully repress.

Deleuze and Guattari reject both of these assumptions. Their opposition to Freud's concept of the Oedipal complex is well known, though it is often mistaken for a wholesale rejection of psychoanalysis, which it is very far from being. Deleuze and Guattari acknowledge the foundational insight of Freud's concept of the unconscious, but suggest things go wrong – that he botches his own invention, in other words – when he proposes the Oedipal complex as the timeless universal truth of the human unconscious. It is not enough, they argue, to either historicize Freud's argument and say that it is only true of twentieth-century Mitteleuropa or to relativize it and say that Oedipus is just a structure and not a real desire, because neither strategy gets to the real problem, which is the idea that the unconscious is organized in this theatrical manner (forbidden desire for the mother coupled with the desire to kill the father).

Deleuze and Guattari are perfectly willing to concede that the Oedipal complex exists and that it is as pervasive in our society as psychoanalysis assumes, but they say this does not mean either that it is a universal truth of human desire or that it is naturally occurring. They reject the idea that the so-called incest taboo, which is at the centre of the Oedipal complex, is in fact a real desire. We cannot assume that just because a desire is banned that a real desire must have preceded the ban. The taboo is merely a lure they argue, designed to make desire feel guilty. The Oedipal complex had to be imposed, they argue, and it had to be imposed for a reason, which they suggest was to capture desire and subordinate it to the demands of power. This is the real reason they are opposed to Oedipus: just as Marx expected exploited workers to 'rise up' once they were shown capitalism is inherently exploitative, so Deleuze and Guattari expect people to reject Oedipus once they realize it inherently serves the interests of the ruling class. In that respect, it is somewhat strange that an avowed Marxist like Slavoj Žižek should fight so hard to maintain the centrality of Oedipus in our lives!

Deleuze and Guattari's rejection of the assumption that it is only because we have internalized societal demands that our desires cause us to suffer is less well known and probably seems contradictory given how often they rail against priests, psychoanalysts and so on, for reinforcing these demands. They do not doubt that Oedipal guilt can cause us to feel self-reproach, but they reject the idea that the Oedipal complex is the sole source of troubling desires. If Deleuze and Guattari sometimes seem to be rejecting psychoanalysis out of hand it is because they think Freud completely misunderstands schizophrenia and the demands it places on those afflicted with the disease. Deleuze and Guattari refer to the demands schizophrenia places on desire as 'becoming' (which I will discuss in more detail in Chapter 3). Ultimately they reject Freud's assumption that schizophrenic deliria can be explained in Oedipal terms on the clinical grounds that it does not have a psychological cause. The actual aetiology of schizophrenia is not fully understood, but it is clear that it is not caused by the Oedipus complex and cannot be cured by means of psychotherapy. Guattari quite pointedly never speaks of 'curing' schizophrenia, or of somehow 'restoring' the patient to their pre-schizophrenic existence. Partly this is because it is impossible, but it also follows a moral perspective which is that there is nothing wrong with being schizophrenic. He often spoke about people's right to be mad. Guattari's approach was to find ways of living well with schizophrenia, that acknowledged both the devastating effects the disease can have as well as the creative possibilities it sometimes opens up. In spite of his interest in the experiments of the anti-psychiatrists, like Laing and Cooper, Guattari did not endorse their methods. La Borde did not resemble Kingsley Hall.[13]

The Transformation of Desire

The body without organs has a complicated history in Deleuze and Guattari's work: it evolved from a negative concept into an affirmative concept over the course of several iterations.[14] One thing that does not change across these various iterations is the fact that the body without organs is the product of the transformation of desire. However it is arrived at, whether spontaneously (*Anti-Oedipus*) or deliberately (*A Thousand Plateaus*), it is always a transformation of desire from something wild and free-flowing into something bounded that harnesses the energy of desire for its own ends. Given that they use Marx's account of capital as a model for the body without organs it is perhaps permissible to describe its coming into being as the desire equivalent of primitive accumulation.

The body without organs does not attract our desire, indeed one of its primary functions is to *repel* desire; rather it captures desire and puts it to work in such a way that we experience it as the cause of our desire.[15] It assumes that desire is both machinic, by which they mean functional, and fragmentary, an endless array of *objets petit a* to borrow Lacan's notion which they explicitly mobilize in their account of desiring-machines. The body without organs captures these disparate desires and corrals them onto a kind of platform such that all future desiring redounds to its benefit. The choice of the word platform here is deliberate because this is exactly how platform capitalism works. Uber is emblematic in this regard – its platform captures millions of trips such that all drivers and passengers pay it a dividend even though it does not itself own cars or employ drivers. The structure of the platform is analogous to the structure of the body without organs as well in that it is very much an instance of what they call a 'peripheral totality': 'it is a whole *of* these particular parts but does not totalize them; it is a unity *of* all these particular parts but does not unify them; rather, it is added to them as a new part fabricated separately.'[16] This is exactly how Uber is constructed, there is no unity of its parts within the framework of any conceivable totality of its parts, but those parts are nevertheless made to function together by the platform for the benefit of the platform.

Deleuze and Guattari's project presupposes that desire in its 'free state', which they associate with the experience of schizophrenia, is tantamount to both the beginning and the end of thought and with that the end of society itself because in their view there is no distinction to be drawn between individual forms of desire and collective or social forms of desire. 'The truth of the matter is that *social production is purely and simply desiring-production itself under determinate conditions*.'[17] In order for society to exist, according to Deleuze and Guattari, desire must be coded, displaced and ultimately repressed, but in its 'free state' it is none of these things, and that is its beauty, its power and its danger. If this sounds Freudian that is because it is. 'The great discovery of psychoanalysis was that of the production of desire, of the production of the unconscious. But once Oedipus entered the picture, this discovery was soon buried [. . .] and an unconscious that was capable of nothing but expressing itself – in myth, tragedy, dreams – was substituted for the productive unconscious.'[18] We can put to one side the practical matters of how desire is coded, repressed and displaced, which are all functions of the assemblage, and note – staying with psychoanalysis for the moment – that for Deleuze and Guattari desire in its productive state constitutes the real, in Lacan's sense of the word.

Far from being impossible, though, as Lacan says of the real, the real for Deleuze and Guattari is where 'everything is possible, everything becomes possible'.[19] However, what this sense of infinite possibility gives with one hand it takes away with the other because the feeling that nothing is impossible is one in which all the certainties we take for granted have been dissolved such that we can no longer distinguish between the true and the false, the good and the bad, and so on. We may feel we can do anything, but that feeling comes at the price of knowing that the same is true of everything else in our world, such that (*pace* Baudelaire) flowers really can be evil. Desire in its 'free state' appears chaotic, inasmuch as it is formless, but as Deleuze and Guattari specify chaos is not defined by the absence of the determination of forms as is commonly supposed, but rather the infinite speed with which new determinations of forms appear and disappear. 'This is not a movement from one determination to the other but, on the contrary, the impossibility of a connection between them, since one does not appear without the other one having already disappeared.'[20]

It is against this background that the therapeutic dimension of the concept of the rhizome becomes apparent because for Deleuze and Guattari 'making a rhizome' means finding a way to connect one's disparate desires together in such a way as to give rise to a platform upon which one can stand up and meet life. When Deleuze and Guattari say of the rhizome that any point on it can and must be connected to any other point, they do not mean either that the rhizome as such already exists, or that the connections it makes already exist.[21] 'In the case of Little Hans, studying the unconscious would be to show how he tries to build a rhizome, with the family house but also with the line of flight of the building, the street, etc.' and it would show that Freud's intervention, via the father, subjectified his affects and left his desire with no escape but that of becoming-animal, which he experienced as shameful.[22]

The act or process of making rhizomes belongs to the order of what psychoanalysis refers to as the self-cure. 'Schizoanalysis, or pragmatics, has no other meaning: Make a rhizome. But you don't know what you can make a rhizome with, you don't know which subterranean stem is effectively going to make a rhizome, or enter a becoming, people your desert. So experiment.'[23] The reason rhizomes must be made – the reason why making them becomes an urgent matter of life and death – is that desire in its pure state is experienced as an incapacity (sometimes terrifying) to form connections of any type, between thoughts, between ideas, between objects and so on, because all of these elements appear and disappear too rapidly for the mind to get any traction on them. Freud himself noted this in his account of the various forms of resistance to analysis he encountered in his patients over the course of his career. 'It would seem that certain subjects have such a *viscous* libido, or on the contrary such a *liquid* one, that nothing succeeds in "taking hold".'[24] It is perhaps worth noting here, too, that the concept of the body without organs is derived in large part from Melanie Klein's notion of the liquid object, which functions as kind of absolute resistance to the importunes of 'objects' (as I have shown elsewhere the phrase is Artaud's, but its analytic sense stems from Klein).[25]

Desiring-production in its pure state can usefully be thought of as a manic, unstoppable energy that gives the subject no rest and undoes all the coordinates by which they would know themselves. Contained by the processes of coding, repression and displacement, it functions as a ground bass, a kind of driving force that one feels, but is not specifically aware of, except as it manifests in the many desiring-machines that give structure to our lives in the form of a variety of things we feel we 'must do'. Desiring-machines have the energy of compulsions, obsessions even, that put desire in motion. But if desiring-production slips its chains, as it always does to varying degrees, then it is experienced as a disruptive, albeit potentially very creative, force. This is the sense in which desiring-production can be seen as a 'breakthrough' as Deleuze and Guattari call it. By the same token, this energy can, in certain circumstances, lead to its opposite, a 'breakdown' in the form of a force of anti-production, which Deleuze and Guattari initially called the body without organs, that manifests as catatonia, or what amounts to the same thing a living death:

> The body without organs is the model of death. As the authors of horror stories have understood so well, it is not death that serves as the model for catatonia, it is catatonic schizophrenia that gives its model to death. Zero intensity. The death model appears when the body without organs repels organs and lays them aside: no mouth, no tongue, no teeth – to the point of self-mutilation, to the point of suicide.[26]

Artaud serves as the model for what this state of being looks like: 'The full body without organs is the unproductive, the sterile, the unengendered, the unconsumable. Antonin Artaud discovered this one day, finding himself with no shape or form whatsoever, right there where he was at that moment.'[27]

This breakdown should not be thought of as the equivalent of the death drive in psychoanalysis, despite the fact they refer to it as an instance of the 'death instinct'.[28] Deleuze and Guattari are very specific about this, the body without organs is not a form of the death drive. It is the model of death, and it may even be experienced as the desire for death, but it is not in itself a death drive. Admittedly, *Anti-Oedipus* is unclear on this issue inasmuch as it frequently mentions the death instinct, but it is very clear in its rejection of the notion of the drive itself, which by implication means they must also reject the existence of a death drive. 'There is no doubt that at this point in history the neurotic, and the pervert, and the psychotic cannot be adequately defined in terms of drives, for drives are simply the desiring-machines themselves. They must be defined in terms of modern territories.'[29] There is no such ambiguity, however, in *A Thousand Plateaus*, which explicitly rejects the notion of the death drive. 'We are not invoking any kind of death drive. There are no internal drives in desire, only assemblages. Desire is always assembled; it is what the assemblage determines it to be.'[30] The concept of the assemblage replaced the desiring-machine, but did not alter its basic meaning; it simply opened the concept onto a much broader field of experiences. Where desiring-machines were largely positioned as pathological, as the active components of the various manifestations of neurosis and psychosis, assemblages span the spectrum from the pathological to the 'normal' (for the want of a better word).

For Deleuze and Guattari, desire is at the forefront of all our interactions with the world and it is always to be understood in terms of production rather than consumption. The world we see is the world desire makes. This is the profound meaning of Deleuze's enigmatic declaration: 'in our universal schizophrenia, *we need reasons to believe in this world*'.[31] It amounts to saying we need reasons to believe in the truth of how we feel, because what we feel is the truth of our world. This truth simultaneously guides us in all our encounters *and* functions as the ground beneath our feet. We constantly doubt the truth of our feelings because they do not always feel like they are *our* feelings; often they feel unbidden, alien, disturbing and strange. These are the feelings Deleuze and Guattari refer to as becomings; their effect on us, on our affect, is said to be deterritorializing because it displaces us from feeling 'at home' in our own world. The extreme form of this feeling of deterritorialization is psychosis, which generally instantiates a 'clean break' between the 'I' we think 'we' are and the intrusive voices that crowd it out. We reterritorialize on these voices because otherwise we would simply disintegrate into disconnected fragments lacking the centring illusion of a 'self'. It is better to be a foreigner, a stranger, a sea bird, a land bird, a tree, a husband, a wife and so on than nothing at all.[32]

Desire is the Cause of Reality

If the notion of 'meeting life' I have used until now to characterize affect's function makes it seem as though affect is ultimately passive, a matter of reception not production (contrary to what I have argued), then that misconception can be laid to rest by turning to Deleuze's 'inversion', as it were, of Kant. Desire, as Deleuze and Guattari define it, borrowing from and effectively inverting Kant, is the *cause of the reality* of the world as we encounter it.[33] This is what Deleuze and Guattari mean by desiring-production. It should not be confused with relativism because the world at issue is the one we engage with – it is the world that we are active in. Deleuze and Guattari reject Kant's argument that the reality desire causes *is merely a psychic reality* and instead insist that what desire produces is the real itself. It is not by chance, they say, that Kant chooses to illustrate his claim that desire causes reality with 'superstitious beliefs, hallucinations, and fantasies' because in his view 'we are well aware that the real object can be produced only by an external causality and external mechanisms' but nonetheless act as though we believe 'in the intrinsic power of desire to create its own object' albeit in an 'unreal, hallucinatory, or delirious form'.[34] As such, 'Kant's critical revolution changes nothing essential'.[35] This was the conclusion Deleuze had already reached in the book he wrote shortly before he met Guattari, *Difference and Repetition*. He says that the much touted break in philosophy, the fabled before and after Kant, essentially amounts to the same thing, i.e. nothing of consequence actually changed.

Of more interest, he argues, is the moment when Kant 'puts rational theology into question' because in that instant 'he introduces a kind of disequilibrium, a fissure or crack in the pure Self of the "I think", an alienation in principle, insurmountable in principle: the subject can henceforth represent its own spontaneity only as that of an Other, and in doing so invoke a mysterious coherence in the last instance which excludes its own – namely, that of the world and God'.[36] It doesn't matter that Kant soon resolves this crisis, Deleuze says, because for 'a brief moment we enter into that schizophrenia in principle which characterizes the highest power of thought, and opens Being directly onto difference'.[37] Ultimately, though, Kant botches his own discovery, according to Deleuze, by designating it as a realm of receptivity, lacking in the power of synthesis.[38] Kant's assumption, according to Deleuze, is that the passive self receives sensations that are already formed, which are then related to a priori forms. In this way he unifies the fractured self that his own thought had put into crisis and rules out the idea that it might be formed step by step and that it might exercise a power of synthesis.[39]

By contrast, Deleuze advocates for a more productive view of how reception works. In contrast to Kant, he holds that 'receptivity [i.e. the domain of affect] must be defined in terms of the formation of local selves or egos, in terms of the passive syntheses of contemplation or contraction, thereby accounting simultaneously for the possibility of experiencing sensations, the power of reproducing them and the value that pleasure assumes as a principle'.[40] We can trace the entire development of schizoanalysis to this moment because it positions the schizophrenic experience (which we might provisionally define, following Foucault – who was in turn inspired by Borges – as 'the stark impossibility of thinking *that*'), as the starting point for how we think about the formation of experience, rather than its endpoint.[41] As Deleuze put it in *Difference and Repetition*, 'schizophrenia is not only a human fact but also a possibility for thought'.[42] Ultimately Deleuze and Guattari postulate that desire is 'the set of passive syntheses that engineer partial objects, flows, and bodies, and that function as units of production. The real is the end product, the result of the passive syntheses of desire as the autoproduction of the unconscious'.[43] It is on this basis that they proclaim that desire 'is a machine, and the object of desire is another machine connected to it'.[44] It is not receptivity, or what we might think of as the surface capacity to experience sensations, that defines the affective domain of the self, but rather the contemplating and contracting machines of the passive syntheses underpinning it which constitute the mainspring of how we experience stimuli. Affect is typically positioned as a response to stimuli, but as Deleuze and Guattari show it is more usefully thought of as that which determines the kind of response we may have to stimuli. We have to be capable of feeling happy for a given stimulus to induce happiness; what we call depression is precisely an absence of a capacity to feel happiness.

From the opening pages of *Anti-Oedipus* Deleuze and Guattari constantly foreground the astonishing variety of ideas, thoughts and desires humans are capable of. Doubtless there is a certain sensationalism in what they do – de Certeau identified a similar tendency in Foucault who, he says, 'traps strange things which he discovers in a past literature and uses these for disturbing our fragile present securities' – but it also lays bare a central problematic with regards the operation of desire.[45] For what interested Deleuze in *Difference and Repetition*, which carried over into his collaborations with Guattari, is precisely the capacity of the mind to produce intensities which not only precede and give shape to thought, but also seem to force 'us' to think in particular ways. If desire is the *cause of the reality* of the world we encounter then the set of passive syntheses are the cogs and springs that like a watch's mechanism make that reality real to us without themselves being seen.

Affect theory treats affect as a form of reception, whereas for Deleuze and Guattari it is an apparatus of production. For affect theory, affect is an attribute of the body, but this is both a diminishment of Spinoza's argument and a weakening of the concept of affect as it functions in Deleuze and Guattari's work. Ultimately, Deleuze's conceptualization of affect as an agency of the mind does not derive from his work on Spinoza. Certainly, it draws on and pays homage to Spinoza, but Spinoza does not hold all the answers to understanding this concept. Rather, it is *Difference and Repetition*, the book that by his own lights marks the beginning of the work he did for himself, that sets out the functional structure of affect as it appears in his collaborations with Guattari. The project he began in *Difference and Repetition*, which he called 'transcendental empiricism', provides the conceptual framework for his collaborative project with Guattari (schizoanalysis). Deleuze summarizes its schema as follows: 'Empiricism truly becomes transcendental, and aesthetics an apodictic discipline, only when we apprehend directly in the sensible that which can only be sensed, the very being of the sensible: difference, potential difference and difference in intensity as the reason behind qualitative diversity.'[46] This realm, which Deleuze does not name in *Difference and Repetition*, but only designates as the object of his inquiries under the banner of transcendental empiricism, is, I want to suggest, *the domain of affect*. This domain is conceived by Deleuze as an 'intense world of differences' which exhibits 'a strange "reason", that of the multiple, chaos and difference (nomadic distributions, crowned anarchies)'.[47]

Deleuze exemplifies this claim with reference to Beckett in a passage that will be familiar to anyone who has read the first chapter of *Anti-Oedipus*. 'Molloy's series of stones, Murphy's biscuits, Malone's possessions – it is always a question of drawing a small difference, a weak generality, from the repetition of elements or the organization of cases. It is undoubtedly one of the more profound intentions of the "new novel" to rediscover, below the level of active syntheses, the domain of passive syntheses which constitute us, the domain of modifications, tropisms and little peculiarities.'[48] These subterranean passive syntheses are not simply microperceptions, they are the working parts of our desiring-machines which, when they're 'working', generate and sustain a specific mode of 'feeling', expressed in terms of attraction and repulsion, which is to say a certain capacity to act. The difference between non-schizophrenics and schizophrenics is that schizophrenics are conscious of and have direct experience of these working parts for themselves. This is what Deleuze and Guattari mean when they say the schizophrenic experiences 'nature as a process of production'.[49] For most of us, thinking and feeling occurs spontaneously, without either conscious effort or awareness; indeed, we are often mystified by our own thoughts and feelings, which is why the psychotherapy industry in all its myriad forms, from self-help books to mindfulness workshops and yoga videos, all the way through to professional clinical care, is thriving.

All forms of psychotherapy assume that the process of thought is essentially orderly, or at least susceptible to being ordered (i.e. that we can know finally why we think *that*), but what schizophrenia demonstrates is that this is not necessarily the case: schizophrenia is profoundly disordering at the level of process. Deleuze and Guattari build their understanding of this aspect of schizophrenia into their account of desire as a machinic process that works precisely by going off the rails altogether. 'Desiring-machines work only when they break down [détraquées, i.e. literally going off the rails], and by continually breaking down [détraquant]'.[50] In this respect, one might treat desiring-machines as a pathological form that in their very productivity disrupts the 'orderly' functioning of the mind. The transition from desiring-machine to assemblage in Deleuze and Guattari's work allowed them to theorize the workings of all forms of desiring, not just those that appear pathological, or off the rails.

One of the less-remarked-upon implications of this transition is the fact that as pivotal as the concept of the passive syntheses is in *Anti-Oedipus* and the books Deleuze completed immediately prior to his collaboration with Guattari, namely *Difference and Repetition* and *The Logic of Sense*, it plays no part in subsequent books. I would argue, though, that just as the desiring-machine morphed into the assemblage, so its internal mechanism – the passive syntheses – morphed into the distinction between the form of content and form of expression which is the basic mechanism of the assemblage. I make this point because I think it helps us to avoid falling into the trap of treating the combination of the form of content and form of expression as simply classificatory tools rather than the working parts of the assemblage. Assemblage theory in many of its iterations has tended to ignore the fact that as Deleuze and Guattari conceive it the assemblage consists of two types of forms: the *form* of content and the *form* of expression. When Deleuze and Guattari say that desire is machinic this is what they are referring to, the process of forming and linking new forms of content and new forms of expression that the concept of the assemblage names. Affect as it is construed by affect theory has neither this power nor this dignity because it is conceptually positioned as something that operates within an existing reality, rather than as a cause of that reality.

It needs to be emphasized here that the assemblage is not and cannot be thought of as a 'collection of contents' to cite but one instance of literally countless examples of this way of thinking about assemblages.[51] That this way of thinking about assemblages has proven to be so enduring is something that baffles me because it is so obviously wrong, not just as a reading of Deleuze and Guattari but as a matter of empirical fact. In the opening pages of *A Thousand Plateaus* Deleuze and Guattari describe the book – their book! – as an assemblage. In what sense is this just a collection of contents? One might say it is just a collection of ink marks on paper (or pixels on a screen), that it is just a collection of letters cobbled together into words, and so on, but would this meaningfully define it as a book? Obviously not. The marks on the page are part of a sign-system, the words are combined according to linguistic systems, and there are conventions of writing and thinking that shape the writing. Without these systems the book could neither be written nor read. It is the particular arrangements of these systems that constitute the content of the assemblage and they cannot be understood as simply a collection of contents because they have an internal logic that decides, at a minimum, what is included and what is excluded from the book. They also create the conditions under which we are able to 'make sense' of the book as something other than just a collection of contents. When we read, it is these organizational aspects of the book that we are essentially trying to discern because that is how we 'make sense' of it. The same is true of all assemblages: they are not collections of contents, they are systems – machines – for producing content. Just as a pile of bolts isn't a machine, so a collection of contents isn't an assemblage.

The Body without Organs

The passive syntheses – i.e. the desiring processes – give rise to a curious, but absolutely vital agency of the mind which Deleuze and Guattari refer to as the body without organs. It appears spontaneously as a direct result of the processes of desire. 'Desiring-machines make us an organism; but at the very heart of this production, within the very production of this production, the body suffers from being organized in this way, from not having some other sort of organization, or no organization at all.'[52] In response to this suffering the 'automata [the desiring processes] stop dead and set free the unorganized mass they once served to articulate'.[53] The result is the body without organs, which in this case is defined as 'the unproductive, the sterile, the unengendered, the unconsumable'.[54] As I have already mentioned, Artaud is credited with its discovery, when one day he found 'himself with no shape or form whatsoever, right there where he was at that moment'.[55] In contemporary psychological terms, this would probably be described as a dissociative state because inasmuch as Artaud no longer recognises his 'self' as 'himself' it is manifestly a form of depersonalization. I imagine Deleuze and Guattari would not find much to disagree with in this diagnosis, but neither would they find it satisfying. This is because in psychology and psychiatry the concept of dissociation is used to frame a mental aberration which needs to be corrected, whereas they regard all schizophrenic symptoms as types of experience that should be understood for themselves in an immanent manner.

This approach acknowledges that schizophrenia cannot be 'cured' in any meaningful sense of the word. Contemporary medicine is constantly experimenting with pharmacological ways of managing certain of the symptoms of schizophrenia, with greater or lesser efficacy, but it cannot cure the disease. At best, drugs can mute the symptoms, tempering the highs and lows, and staving off some of the more distressing hallucinations. But the truth is, once schizophrenia appears there is no going back to a pre-schizophrenic state, so the therapeutic approach has to be ameliorative rather than restorative. As Guattari argues throughout his work, it is a matter of finding ways to live with schizophrenia that respect the specificities of the disease, particularly its ways of seeing and thinking (its unique regime of signs). This is difficult because schizophrenia is not susceptible to the standard psychotherapeutic practices of psychoanalysis – the 'talking cure' (as Breuer's patient Anna O famously called it) doesn't work with schizophrenics. Schizophrenia is organically caused, although no one really knows its precise aetiology. As such there are no 'triggering' psychological moments or encounters one can 'work through' in order to deal with the symptoms and thereby lay them to rest. This is the basic point of their critique of Freud's analysis of the Wolfman. Freud, they say, doesn't listen to what schizophrenics actually say because he is constantly trying to decode their statements in terms of the Oedipal rubric he devised. 'Talk as he might about wolves, howl as he might like a wolf, Freud does not even listen; he glances at his dog and answers "It's daddy".[56] This is why Deleuze and Guattari always insist on the idea that desire is a form of autoproduction, which can only be understood for itself and not as the representation of something else (i.e. Oedipus). Schizoanalysis is conceived in precisely these terms: its goal is to 'map' the autoproductions of the unconscious in an immanent fashion. Hence their prolific invention of new concepts to map these ways of thinking, acting and being that do not follow the standard precepts of what is regarded as 'normal' or 'reasonable'.

The concept of the body without organs exemplifies this point perfectly. Where psychology sees an aberration, a dissociative state, a glitch in the normal way of being, schizoanalysis sees a new form of psychical agency whose coordinates are not yet fully known: the body without organs. We can begin to understand this agency more fully by looking at how it works. 'The full body without organs is produced as antiproduction, that is to say it intervenes within the process [of desiring] for the sole purpose of rejecting any attempt to impose on it any sort of triangulation implying that it was produced by the parents. How could this body have been produced by parents, when by its very nature it is such eloquent witness of its own self-production, of its own engendering of itself?'[57] The body without organs has 'nothing whatsoever to do with the body itself, or with an image of the body. It is the body without an image'.[58] Its principal function is to connect the syntheses of production (i.e. the processes of desire, desiring-machines, assemblages and so on) with a form of antiproduction which introduces resistance into the flow of desire. Under certain circumstances, the desiring-machines and the body without organs they give rise to enter into a state of conflict such that their productions are felt to be 'so many nails piercing the flesh, so many forms of torture'.[59] When this happens the body without organs repels the desiring-machines by initiating a counterflow.

In *Anti-Oedipus*, as we have seen, the body without organs arises spontaneously in response to the processes set in motion by the desiring-machine and essentially functions as form of resistance (in the psychoanalytic sense). Once the body without organs is formed, however, it functions in such a way as to make it seem that it is the origin of all desiring processes. Now, instead of being a repulsion machine it becomes an attraction machine, and the desiring-machines (organs) that had once been so many nails piercing the flesh are reborn as the agents of the body without organs. 'The body without organs is not God, quite the contrary. But the energy that sweeps through it is divine, when it attracts to itself the entire process of production.'[60] In *A Thousand Plateaus* the body without organs must be produced: it still arises spontaneously (in the sense that it cannot be purposely constructed, hence the need for constant experimentation), but it is no longer concerned solely with resisting the imprecations of the desiring-machines (assemblages), though that remains a crucial driving force. It arises wherever someone gets tired of feeling the way they do and tries to do something about it. The effect of its appearance, however, is the same in *A Thousand Plateaus* as it is in *Anti-Oedipus*. It initiates a paradigm shift in the process of desire. *Anti-Oedipus* theorizes this in terms of the transformation of paranoid desiring-machines into fetishes functioning as quasi-causes of desire.[61] *A Thousand Plateaus* theorizes it in more pragmatic terms: something is produced and something is made to circulate.

The Dreary Parade

By their own admission, most of the examples Deleuze and Guattari give of the body without organs – a 'dreary parade of sucked-dry, catatonicized, vitrified, sewn-up bodies' as they put it – relate to what I have called the 'negative' dimension of the concept.[62] In my view, though, this 'dreary parade' obscures what is essential because it is hard to see its analytic side when it is so effectively camouflaged by such a bewildering array of astonishing descriptions of the different ways and means people have experimented with to make themselves a body without organs. Deleuze and Guattari's prime exhibit in this respect is masochism, which they say is poorly understood in terms pain or phantasy.[63] The masochist's procedures, which they enumerate in some detail ('You may tie me down on the table, ropes drawn tight . . .' and so on), constitutes a two-part programme for constructing a body without organs and making something – intensities – circulate. 'What is certain is that the masochist has made himself a BwO under such conditions that the BwO can no longer be populated by anything but intensities of pain, *pain waves* [. . .] The masochist is looking for a type of BwO that only pain can fill, or travel over, due to the very conditions under which the BwO was constituted.'[64] A programme is required to create the specific conditions required to enable a specific type of body without organs to come into being and another – even if it is the same set of actions – is required to set it motion. Deleuze and Guattari are very careful to say this should not be thought in terms of physical pleasure or the satisfaction of a fantasy, indeed pleasure and satisfaction are said to get in the way of what the masochist is really trying to do. Deleuze and Guattari also reject the idea central to the psychoanalytic account of masochism that the masochist somehow seeks to convert pain into pleasure. The masochist uses suffering, they say, 'not to achieve pleasure, but to untie the psuedobond between desire and pleasure as an extrinsic measure'.[65] For this reason, pleasure has to be postponed for as long as possible because 'it interrupts the continuous process of positive desire'.[66]

If we take a more abstract view here and X-ray out the 'dreary parade' of the specific content of Deleuze and Guattari's case studies (to borrow a phrase and procedure from Jameson, who applies it to the discussion of sexuality in Freud's hermeneutic structures) then we are left with two basic functional components in the structure of the body without organs. (1) Regardless of how it is produced, whether by deliberate experimentation or as a reaction to an intolerable experience, *it takes the form of something unengendered*, with the character of what phenomenology calls the 'always already'. (2) As such, it always appears to the beholder to be the actual origin of the thought, impulse, desire, idea and so on that compels a given behaviour or way of thinking. In effect, *it is the autoproduction of the condition of possibility for action*. This action can vary in scale from that of the individual experimenter – 'drug users, masochists, schizophrenics, lovers'[67] – to that of society itself. 'If we wish to have some idea of the forces that the body without organs exerts [...] we must first establish a parallel between desiring-production and social production.'[68] Ultimately, as I mentioned earlier, they argue that social production is simply desiring-production under determinate conditions. Thus, all 'forms of social production, like those of desiring-production, involve an unengendered non-productive attitude, an element of antiproduction coupled with the process, a full body that functions as a socius [...] This is the body that Marx is referring to when he says that it is not the product of labour, but rather appears as its natural or divine presupposition.'[69]

The body without organs is the space of desire itself as a field of pure possibility.[70] This is why it is divine. The key to understanding the body without organs, in my view, is to see it as one of the crucial ways that a 'capacity to act' is formed and sustained. It sometimes envisages this space of this 'capacity to act' as a desert plain across which nomadic 'bands of intensities' move, thereby causing 'things to happen', and other times as an egg whose potential to develop cannot be foreseen from its current state (one cannot look at a yolk and predict a chicken will form), but what is crucial is that it is not conceived as a given. It is an acquired agency, rather than something we are born with. As such, at the level of the individual it can usefully be thought of as a form of disposition and productively compared with *stimmung* (in Heidegger's sense) and *habitus* (in Bourdieu's sense), without any implication that it is therefore the same as either.

Disposition is a property of the body without organs. It manifests as a specific capacity to feel and act in one way, but not another, and what amounts to the same thing, a willingness to do one thing, but not another.

I have often thought that it is the work of Philip K. Dick rather than Artaud which best exemplifies this aspect of the body without organs. In *Do Androids Dream of Electric Sheep?* there is a nice scene (strangely absent from *Blade Runner*) in which one of the characters uses a device known as the 'Penfield mood organ' which enables its user to dial up the required mood for a given activity (e.g. 'desire to watch TV, no matter what is on').[71] This is exactly the function of the body without organs: it is the foundation of everything that we desire to do. This is why when the body without organs zeroes out, as it does in Artaud's case, it is a disaster which should be regarded as a clinical emergency.

The body without organs 'is desire; it is that which one desires and by which one desires'.[72] It is not *a* desire; it is not *a* desire for this particular thing that we somehow lack – a new car or a new love; it is rather the point at which all desires, conflicting or otherwise, join together and lose their distinction. 'It is only there that the BwO reveals itself for what it is: connection of desires, conjunction of flows, continuum of intensities.'[73] Making a body without organs means consciously constructing the inner resources needed to have *a* 'capacity to act'. I have phrased it this way to highlight the fact that 'capacity to act' does not refer to a specific capability; it is rather the precondition of being able to do anything whatsoever. Sometimes this means finding a way out of a black hole (i.e. depression) and at other times it means clearing a route through an overly complicated set of deeply felt constrictions as to what one can and cannot do (i.e. anxiety). This returns us to, and deepens our understanding of, the 'rhizome'. In the case of black holes, the rhizome refers to the set of branching possibilities available at each moment of the day as one moves through one's daily life. To get up off the couch, or not; to go for a run, or not; to talk to that person, or not; and so on. The rhizomatic choice is the one that leads out of the black hole, rather than the one that leaves you there. In other words, the rhizome isn't a concept that licenses doing anything you want. There is an underlying principle of selection, which is always to get going, to keep going, to get unstuck, to find a way forward, onward and outward, to leave the black hole behind and find a clear space where one feels able to act.

The 'opposite' of depression is not happiness per se but rather the restoration of a certain 'capacity to act' that enables one to do things that previously felt impossible, such as getting off the couch, going for a run, talking to someone and so on. Getting off the couch, going for a run, talking to someone are all instances of choices that overcome a certain affective inertia and break with a previous pattern. Such choices are not always easy to make, for a variety of reasons; sometimes, too, the rhizomatic choice isn't obvious or even visible because one is enmeshed in a web of constrictions (rather than stuck in a black hole) that are like so many striations disfiguring the smooth space of our 'capacity to act'. We can't get off the couch because we might miss our favourite TV show; we can't go for a run because we're not fit enough; we can't talk to a someone because we haven't spoken to them in ages and wouldn't know what to say; and so on. The list of reasons why we can't act can proliferate to such an extent that we feel imprisoned by them. We don't stop being who we are just because we managed to get off the couch and go for a run one day.

This capacity to act needs to be nurtured and sustained through the creation of highly specific assemblages, which very often take the form of new habits. Going for a run once can become going for a run every day. And generally, it is only within the space opened up by the assemblages we manage to immerse ourselves in that the capacity to act is felt. Becoming the sort of person who goes for a daily run where previously one had been utterly sedentary does not mean that one has thereby resolved any of the other difficulties that draw one into a black hole or leave one constricted by too many striations. In extreme cases, the body without organs can itself become toxic because, although it confers a capacity to act, the action itself is like a trap, keeping one stuck within a highly specific framework that steadily erodes one's connection with the other aspects of one's life (Lauren Berlant captures this state of being perfectly in her concept of cruel optimism).[74] As such we must always be careful to evaluate the 'healthfulness' of our bodies without organs. One of the key reasons I felt the need to put brackets around Deleuze's engagement with Spinoza is that it has always seemed to me that affect theory's understandable, but ultimately shortsighted, focus on the word 'affect' in Deleuze and Guattari's work missed what was essential, namely that Deleuze and Guattari have their own theory of affect which begins with the body without organs. But as I will show in the next chapter, the body without organs is a component part of our affect, not the whole story.

3 *THAT* PLANE WORKS FOR ME

The history of ideas should never be continuous; it should be wary of resemblances, but also of descents or filiations; it should be content to mark the thresholds through which an idea passes, the journey it takes that changes its nature or object.[1]

In 1977, the Belgian singer Roger Jouret, going by the name of Plastic Bertrand, had an unlikely worldwide radio and dancefloor hit with a song in French called 'Ça plane pour moi'. Combining elements of both punk and disco, 'Ça plane pour moi' is pure bubble-gum pop with an infectious chorus tag line (the title of the song) that even people who don't know any French, which is of course the majority of its global listeners, happily sang along to. For those who do know French it was a deliciously insouciant counterpoint to a period in France Guattari described as the 'winter years'. I mention this because it has often amused me to think of Plastic Bertrand as an avid reader of Deleuze and Guattari since the title is completely consistent with their thought. It's message is something like, and this is obviously a very free translation, find the plane (of immanence) that works for you and you'll be content. That, I would argue, is exactly what Deleuze and Guattari are saying in their work: it is not the search for enjoyment (in the Lacanian sense), much less pleasure (in either the Freudian or Foucauldian sense), that motivates us, it is rather the search for a very specific state of the plane of immanence that compels us. This plane is not intrinsically good or bad, it can compel people in the direction of fascism just as easily as it can send them towards charitable work and selflessness. The key point, though, is that it is compelling. We will have occasion to inquire more specifically into the exact constitution of the plane of immanence, particularly its compelling nature, but for now it will be sufficient to note that it has three domains of action: perception, thought and sensibility. How we see the world, how we think about the world, and how we feel about the world are all shaped by the plane of immanence. If, as we discussed in the previous chapter, affect precedes our encounter with the world, if it isn't a simple response to stimulus, then how and under what conditions do our ways of seeing, thinking and feeling vary? That answer, as we'll see, has to do with the composition of the plane of immanence.

The Assemblage and the Body without Organs

If it is the search for a very specific state of the plane of immanence that compels us in our daily lives to do the things we do, then it becomes possible to use this as a hermeneutic framework for the way we understand assemblages because all assemblages have the dual function of generating and sustaining a specific body without organs. In this sense it serves the same structural purpose as lack in Lacan and Oedipus in Freud, but offers a different, much less deterministic framework that still gives us an analytic model for understanding human behaviour. In effect, it poses a new problem. This framework is implicit in the opening pages of *Anti-Oedipus* when they say that the essential problem of schizoanalysis is: 'Given a certain effect, what machine is capable of producing it?'[2] What they do not state explicitly at this point, though it becomes clear later on, is that the effect in question is the production of a body without organs. This is necessarily the case because, as we have seen, the instantiation of a body without organs is an inevitable effect of desiring-production. When Deleuze and Guattari stipulate that desire is productive, this is what they mean: desire produces a body without organs which becomes, in turn, the basis of all future desiring-processes (i.e. perception, thought, sensibility).

The model for this is capital. At a certain point, the accumulation of wealth not only becomes self-propelling, it becomes self-enabling, which is to say it becomes its own condition of possibility. As Marx puts it, 'Capital thus becomes a very mystic being since all of labour's social productive forces appear to be due to capital, rather than labour as such, and seem to issue from the womb of capital itself.'[3] The crucial point to note here is that Deleuze and Guattari insist a distinction be made between the creation of a body without organs and its operation. It is not made in the same way that it works. The role of the assemblage varies between these two moments of production and operation: in the first instance its role is to bring the body without organs into existence, then its role switches over to one of maintaining and sustaining the body without organs. In the latter phase it also reaps a return on the original investment, which Deleuze and Guattari explicitly refer to as surplus value. *Anti-Oedipus* is built around the idea that desire invests in certain types of desiring-machines which gives rise to a kind of accumulation of wealth of the capital variety, such that the body without organs is generated, and we earn surplus value on that investment.[4] But in contrast to psychoanalysis in all its forms, Deleuze and Guattari do not envisage this surplus value in terms of cathexis or discharge. The return on investment is not pleasure, it is the field of immanence of our desire that we reap, i.e. the body without organs, as an essential component of what I call the psychical agency of affect. We invest our desire in such a way as to create and sustain a psychical platform that enables us to meet the day. Individual bodies without organs are component parts of this platform and (as I will discuss below) they're not always compatible. Desiring-production has one goal: the production of a sustainable field of immanence of our desire, from which we reap the reward of seeing, thinking about and responding to the world 'in our own way'.

We can see the importance of this proposition for assemblage theory in two ways: first, by looking at examples of assemblage theory which exclude the body without organs from consideration, and second, by looking at examples of assemblage theory which include the body without organs. On the negative side of the ledger, as it were, there are two obvious examples, DeLanda and Bennett, neither of whom make a place for the body without organs in their account of the concept of the assemblage. If we ask the simple question, what purpose do assemblages serve, the answer in both cases is that it has no purpose, no real reason for existing. For DeLanda, all assemblages do is get bigger, while for Bennett they do nothing at all except name a state of affairs defined by the interconnectedness of a great many things. There is no analytic advantage in either model in naming something an assemblage because there is no underpinning problematic: DeLanda does not ask what drives the growth of the assemblage (it is simply a spontaneous effect of the interaction of its components), or even what the point of the growth is, and Bennett simply treats the assemblage as an achieved fact rather than a dynamic problem. Both attribute causality to non-subjective factors, i.e. the property of the materials, thereby eradicating desire from their models altogether. As I have argued elsewhere, Deleuze and Guattari take precisely the opposite course. For our purposes here it is important to note two things: in both cases, the assemblage does not generate anything besides itself, i.e. a body without organs (in Bennett's case it doesn't even do this because on her model the assemblage is an inert collection of contents), or provide a return on investment. In DeLanda's model, this problem is exacerbated by the fact that the assemblage itself is said not to be causal.[5]

As we have seen, though, for Deleuze and Guattari the assemblage is causal: it produces and sustains the body without organs. The assemblage's specific causality, as Deleuze and Guattari put it, manifests as a line of deterritorialization that intersects with other types of causality.[6] If we follow their model – the positive side of the ledger – and ask what kind of a body without organs a specific assemblage is producing then we begin to shift things into an analytic mode. For example, DeLanda treats the assemblage known as the market as though it is a naturally occurring phenomenon, which plainly it isn't since not every human society in history has had one.[7] This is not simply a matter of leaving out the 'historical details behind the assembly of local marketplaces into regional markets', as DeLanda puts it; it is far more fundamental than that because it relates to the desirability of the assemblage itself and the body without organs it generates. If the market is an assemblage, and I agree that it is, then its components are not simply stalls in marketplaces, or goods being shipped from distant places, these are merely the incidental facts of a market already in operation. The actual components of the market assemblage are not material at all. As Deleuze and Guattari show in their account of the origins of capital there are several 'actual factors' underpinning the market: the idea of exchange itself, which even without money entails a mental abstraction and social agreement; it also entails an idea of profit, that every exchange yields surplus value for the parties entering into the agreement – each one thinks they are getting something more than what they had; markets treat exchanges as elastic, prices can fluctuate according to external factors such as supply and demand, inherent scarcity of a given object, changing fashions, actual need and so on. My point, which I have made before, is that the assemblage is not primarily material and cannot be understood in the absence of desire.

As I argued in Chapter 1, new materialism and vital materialism can and should be seen as symptomatic of a larger trend which Jameson usefully describes as the de-Marxification of theory.[8] While I'm flattered by the work Stephen Jay and Timothy Acott have done to frame my disagreements with DeLanda as a dispute between two different ways of conceiving the concept of the assemblage I want to insist that this debate is not simply about the correct way to read Deleuze and Guattari.[9] Rather, as Andreas Malm's *Fossil Capital* nicely adumbrates for us, it turns on the much larger issue of whether one believes that materials give rise to social structures or social structures appropriate materials. For instance, it has long been argued that the superiority of coal as an energy source compared to burning wood meant that the uptake of coal power was inevitable and that once that superiority was harnessed the Industrial Revolution was inevitable. Yet historically that is not the case. As Malm argues, coal was burned in Britain in Roman times, but it was not until the nineteenth century that the Industrial Revolution began in earnest, so the material was not sufficient by itself. Similarly, the invention of the coal-burning steam-powered engine in 1784, which many people take as the start date of the Anthropocene, did not by itself launch the Industrial Revolution. As Malm argues, reiterating Jameson's point quoted in the introduction, it is social relations that create the conditions needed for materials to become 'drivers' of change.[10]

Deleuze and Guattari take exactly the same line: the social machine always precedes the mechanical machine in their work. The transhumants follow materials not because they have to, but because they want to: their form of nomadism is a social structure, a mode of existence, not a side effect of the discovery of certain materials. De-Marxification, as Jameson calls it, manifests as the attempt to avoid this line of reasoning by reversing the argument and making it seem that it is materials themselves that are the real drivers of both technological innovation and social formation. The falsity of this argument can be demonstrated in any number of ways, so I will limit myself to just three points. First, as we have seen, as important as coal is to the Industrial Revolution, it took literally centuries to have its effect, so how do we explain this lag if materials are the cause? Second, given that coal was widely available throughout Europe, why was it that it was only in Great Britain that it sparked an Industrial Revolution? What material-only explanation can be offered? Moreover, why was it the manufacture of textiles that spawned the Industrial Revolution and not some other commodity? By extension, we can also ask: why not China (as Deleuze and Guattari put it, following Etienne Balasz), which had coal and a much larger population and consequently a much greater potential market for textiles?[11] Lastly, given that the world is literally becoming inhospitable to human life because of global warming, why don't we stop burning fossil fuels? If matter is as decisive in driving action as we are given to believe then surely the material fact of an overheating planet would be sufficient to prompt action and yet the contrary has been the case. There is widespread denial and downplaying of the material facts of climate change, suggesting that matter is not decisive at all. The replacement energy technology already exists and has done for centuries – wind turbines and water wheels are thousands of years old – so why hasn't it prompted us to switch? What material-only explanation can be given? As Malm shows, no answers to such questions are forthcoming.

The non-material answer to these questions is capital in Marx's sense. As we have already seen, capital is in fact Deleuze and Guattari's model for the body without organs. Capital, as Marx defines it, is 'retroactive' in its effects. Capital is the product of labour – that's Marx's point – but when accumulation reaches a certain level it becomes self-propelling such that labour becomes dependent on its existence. At that point wealth begets wealth more or less independently of labour – think of how hedge funds work: they have such huge resources at their disposal they can effectively hold entire nations to ransom, as happened during the Global Financial Crisis of 2008. So-called financialization is, in this sense, a body-without-organs effect, rather than an assemblage effect, because it refers to a process whereby the dollar value of the corporation is more important than its actual earnings. Under these conditions, giant companies like Tesla are valued many times over what they actually earn, which gives it a power in the marketplace that is out of proportion to its worth: this power, if you will, is the body without organs in person, as Deleuze and Guattari like to put it. This power manifests as 'growth', which appears to be an 'emergent property' of the corporation's activities, but isn't because in fact it depends on external factors, namely the valuation other corporations – hedge funds principally – place on it. So growth is a retroactive effect which the company claims is the product of its labours, when in reality it is an attribute bestowed upon it from the outside.

As far as I'm aware, Deleuze and Guattari do not explicitly link the body without organs to Freud's notion of the retroactive effect ('Nachträglichkeit'), but it shares many of its principal characteristics. Its effects are always exerted after the fact. The body without organs comes into being alongside our desiring activity, but it is not – strictly speaking

– the product of our desire. It captures our desire and focalizes it in such a way that afterwards we feel that is what we wanted all along. In that moment, the body without organs functions as a way of seeing, thinking and feeling that shapes how we see the world. The importance of this point is perhaps best seen in terms of the way it changes how we should think about the assemblage. I will illustrate this with a necessarily brief discussion of neoliberalism, which I would like to suggest should be grasped as a body without organs. Neoliberalism is, of course, a highly contested term and it is not my intention to either survey the various accounts of it or try to adjudicate between them, much less sort out the differences between national iterations of it. For my purposes, Wendy Brown's comprehensive summary in *Undoing the Demos* is sufficient as a starting point:

> Neoliberalism is most commonly understood as enacting an ensemble of economic policies in accord with its root principle of affirming free markets. These include deregulation of industries and capital flows; radical reduction in welfare state provisions and protections for the vulnerable; privatized and outsourced public goods, ranging from education, parks, postal services, roads, and social welfare to prisons and militaries; replacement of progressive with regressive tax and tariff schemes; the end of wealth redistribution as an economic or social-political policy; the conversion of every human need or desire into a profitable enterprise, from college admissions preparation to human organ transplants, from baby adoptions to pollution; from avoiding lines to securing legroom on an airplane; and [. . .] the financialization of everything and the increasing dominance of finance capital over productive capital in the dynamics of everyday life.[12]

If for argument's sake we took this litany to be a 'collection of contents' (as one finds in Bennett's work) of some kind neoliberalism assemblage then the obvious question we would want to ask is: What explains this state of affairs? The enumeration of a collection of contents one perceives to be connected in some way is a starting point, not an endpoint, and analysis only really begins at the point at which one seeks to uncover the nature of the connections between a given set of contents (as we'll see, this means asking about the plane of immanence and plane of organization).

The assumption that the 'whole' – as DeLanda puts it – emerges as a consequence of the interaction between the parts is clearly false as this example makes apparent. First as a matter of logic, it presupposes the very thing it is meant to explain, namely the existence of the whole – the interaction between the parts of a whole can only be considered an after-effect of the emergence of the whole; second, as a matter of empirical fact – the privatization of schools (to take only one example) did not occur because of an interaction between schools and free markets, or else it would have happened a century sooner. Rather, it happened because an idea – privatization – or what Deleuze and Guattari call a formalized function spread like a toxic virus from one institution to another, causing the organized form of education to be destratified as an affair of the state and subject formation and restratified in the organized form of economic opportunity. It follows from this that we should not assume that it is the collection itself that constitutes the assemblage. One of the crucial errors of new materialism has been to mistake the 'whole' for the assemblage when, as we've seen, the 'whole' is in fact the body without organs, a concept that DeLanda simply ignores.

Brown's list contains several different types of assemblages, so the question might be reframed in terms of whether or not they have anything in common. What, if anything, passes between them? Here, I think it is worth returning (briefly) to Foucault's analysis of discipline, which Deleuze and Guattari take up as one of their handful of worked-out examples of an assemblage. Following Foucault we've become so accustomed to the idea that schools are like prisons that we have forgotten how startling an idea this really is! We've also forgotten that asylums, schools, hospitals, prisons, factories and so on were not initially alike, each one had its own way of doing things – they were distinct forms with equally distinct sets of internal formalized functions. Foucault's attention was drawn to these institutions precisely because in his archival research he detected a convergence between them such that unalike institutions (schools, churches, prisons and so on) began to exhibit unexpected similarities. Foucault's hypothesis is that as each of these organized forms became aware of the transformative potential of the panopticon apparatus (formalized function) they adopted it and adapted its principles to the needs of their specific forms. This can be seen by comparing hospitals and prisons – both adopted panopticism, but to very different ends. For the prison it was a matter of using surveillance to modify the behaviour of the prisoners, but for the hospital it was to maximize the visibility of disease processes and increase the efficiency of care.

The similarity between hospitals and prisons was not at the level of organized forms, it was rather at the level of formalized functions, or 'segments' (as Deleuze initially called them in his review of *Discipline and Punish*). There is correspondence between these forms, but they remain irreducible to one another inasmuch that 'care', for instance, has not always been the preserve of hospitals and can be found at work in such diverse institutions as churches and schools. But, as Deleuze also notes, it is not necessarily the same 'care' that is found in each of these institutions. 'Care' can also be found in the prison in the form of ideas such as rehabilitation and redemption. Some assemblage components move as 'hard' segments, meaning they stay the same wherever they are found (e.g. surveillance), while others are 'supple' segments, that vary from instance to instance, while still retaining sufficient identity to be recognizable (e.g. 'care'). Surveillance of a street or prison yard or classroom is performed using essentially the same technology (eyes) and with essentially the same intent (modification of behaviour); but care varies quite considerably from institution to institution – pastoral care of the needs of the soul is not the same as medical care of the body – but each iteration nonetheless retains sufficient 'family resemblance' (to use Wittgenstein's useful notion) with all the other iterations such that it is meaningful to use the same word across all instances. Deleuze makes a methodological point here that is worth underscoring and that has to do with the nature and function of what is referred to here as a 'segment'. A segment is *any* operative component of an assemblage. There is no specific restriction on what type of 'thing' may be a segment, indeed practically anything can be, including other assemblages. But it's important to remember that assemblages are not composed of material things – it is constituted by connections and conjugations between organized forms and formalized functions.

This, in turn, raises the issue of how and under what circumstances does coadaptation occur (as Deleuze calls it) between the two different forms (organized forms and formalized functions). As an aside here, one could do worse than to think of the assemblage in these terms as the 'trigger', if you will, that brings about the coadaptation of organized forms and formalized functions. In order to resolve this conundrum Deleuze turns to Hjelmslev. Coadaptation is possible, Deleuze argues, because 'we can conceive of pure matter and pure functions, abstracting the forms which embody them'.[13] Evident here is Hjelmslev's idea that all words and things (or what Deleuze and Guattari refer to more simply as matter) are essentially meaningless until they've been captured by a form (at which point matter is transformed into substance). This way of mapping things allows us to see that panopticism is both a defining characteristic of the contemporary prison *and* an apparatus or *dispositif* that in varying ways can be seen at work in any institution where managing human behaviour is crucial (public streets, train stations, shopping malls, theme parks and so on, none of which necessarily share any other formal characteristics with prisons).[14] Panopticism is in this respect a supple segment which unlike prison walls and prison cells has been able to migrate readily into a wide variety of institutional settings (not forgetting of course that the idea did not originate with prisons, but in fact derives from the central dome of the Orthodox churches Bentham saw in Russia which are typically covered with the image of Christ *Pantokrator*, or the 'Ruler of All' that functions as an allegory of the idea that God is all-seeing).[15]

The retroactive effect I spoke of above that points to the operation of the body without organs, rather than an assemblage, or assemblages, is evident almost everywhere one looks today in discussions about neoliberalism. As several commentators have observed, drawing on Bernard Harcourt, neoliberalism is a counter-revolution that occurred in the absence of a revolution – its proponents advocate for neoliberal policies to 'remedy' a revolutionary socialist agenda that never materialized anywhere in the so-called first world.[16] In other words, neoliberalism did not emerge as the consequence of the interaction between elements in the economy, it was deliberately constructed and imposed from without and in the absence of the very thing it was said to be against. And that is still its modus operandi today: it presents itself as a solution to problems its own policies create but which it continues to blame on a non-existent leftist hegemony. Although I don't have the space to argue this point fully here, I do want to make the observation, as a kind of caution I suppose, that policies cannot by themselves be construed as assemblages – they are components of an assemblage. Within an assemblage policy functions as a kind of coding-machine which assigns meanings and values to the other components of the assemblage and at the same time opens up a forum of discussion about the meanings and values it has assigned. Policies are not assemblages in and of themselves because like all performatives, which they can certainly be classified as, they require certain felicity conditions to be met before they can have their effect: for instance, neoliberal policies on taxation are meaningless in the absence of a taxation system and indeed something of the order of an economy. Moreover the policies are not by themselves self-legitimating, they need to be connected to a range of other expressive components in order to be accepted and 'normalized'.

Neoliberalism was first and foremost an ideology (i.e. body without organs) that celebrated 'business' as the 'highest' form of government. In other words, in classic body without organs fashion, it emerged long after the idea of government but presented itself as the origin of good governance. As Laval and Dardot put it, 'neoliberal policies are not adaptions to objective logics imposed from without, like natural laws, even if they present themselves as such. Instead they strive to construct situations and intensify dynamics that *indirectly* compel governments to accept the consequences of their own previous policies'.[17] It is only against this background that the devastating consequences of neoliberal policies can be understood because at every turn, even as welfare services are slashed and people are deliberately made to suffer deprivation in the midst of abundance, this shibboleth is trotted out as not merely justification for the heartless policies enacted but as a righteous pronouncement that a long-standing error of governance had been corrected. That it is a body without organs effect, rather than an assemblage effect, can be seen in the way neoliberalism always functions as a form of legitimation. It is for this reason that it can and does thrive on chaos and crisis. Indeed, as Laval and Dardot argue, 'crisis has become the main lever for reinforcing neoliberal policies. Thus, to paraphrase Churchill, it might be said that for neoliberalism, every obstacle is an opportunity'.[18]

A Tale of Two Planes

The search for the plane that works for us goes by the way of our bodies without organs, of which we usually have several, but only reaches its destination when we put together the resources required to construct the plane of immanence. The plane is not fully formed and waiting for us at the end of a long dark tunnel, it has to be cobbled together by finding the means of connecting all our different bodies without organs into a single composite, which has to be maintained:

> Castaneda describes a long process of experimentation (it makes little difference whether it is with peyote or other things): let us recall for the moment how the Indian forces him to find a 'place', already a difficult operation, then to find 'allies', and then gradually to give up

interpretation, to construct flow by flow and segment by segment lines of experimentation, becoming-animal, becoming-molecular, etc.[19]

Castenada interests Deleuze and Guattari, despite any scepticism they might have about the actual existence of his Indian informant Don Juan, because his work encapsulates a great deal of what they are trying say about schizoanalysis. For instance, with regards to the passage just quoted they say, 'the BwO is all of that: necessarily a Place, necessarily a Plane, necessarily a Collectivity (assembling elements, things, plants, animals, tools, people, powers, and fragments of all of these; for it is not "my" body without organs, instead the "me" (*moi* [ego]) is on it, or what remains of me, unalterable and changing in form, crossing thresholds)'.[20] I have quoted this at length because in addition to providing a useful account of the specific nature of the body without organs it is also allows me to segue to a crucial clarification of Deleuze and Guattari's terminology that I now need to make. I have often said that the body without organs and the plane of immanence are synonymous, but I must now admit that this is imprecise. Although the passage just quoted would seem to bear out my claim it is nevertheless inexact, although not therefore inaccurate, because while the body without organs and the plane of immanence share several key characteristics – they are both instances of the field of desire we know as affect – one is singular and the other is collective. The 'plane is the totality of the full BwO's that have been selected (there is no positive totality including the cancerous or empty bodies)'.[21] The body without organs is an element of the plane of immanence, but this should not be construed to mean it is a fragment of a previously existing whole. It has agency in its own right which is independent of the plane of immanence. However, it is also capable of combining with other bodies without organs in such a way as to form the plane of immanence. This formation should not be regarded as synthetic, the individual bodies without organs do not lose their identity or their agency; rather, it has the character of a mixture.

There are two implications that follow from this point I want to single out at this stage. First, we usually have more than one body without organs, one could even say it is actually unhealthy to have only one body without organs. This is not always clear in Deleuze and Guattari's account of the body without organs. It often seems as though they are saying we only have one, but this cannot be the case if the plane is the totality of all bodies without organs. They also seem to be saying that in instances where there is only one body without organs that should be regarded as a pathological situation. Second, not all bodies without organs can be combined with all other bodies without organs, some instances are mutually exclusive (e.g. one cannot be a drug-user and a non-drug-user at the same time). This means affect does not consist of a single element by itself, which is how 'pop' psychology tends to view it, but is *constituted by a multiplicity of elements functioning together.* The principal goal of all experimental bodies without organs is precisely to find a way of connecting the existing bodies without organs that comprise one's affect in such a way that one can reach the plane of immanence and find a state of mutual reciprocity between the competing demands our desires impose upon us. Where people go wrong, Deleuze and Guattari argue, is in thinking that the only way to bring about the state of mutual reciprocity between their various bodies without organs is by obliterating the incompatible elements, but as they repeatedly emphasize one does not reach the plane of immanence in this way. Experimentation means finding ways to blend the apparently incompatible, not simply by eliminating the incompatible (e.g. find the drugs that work, that enhance one's life without risking it, rather than eliminate all drugs – as Deleuze and Guattari often say, it all comes down to an art of doses). Getting this wrong can have deadly consequences and they are very explicit in stating the need for caution.[22]

The one absolute rule Deleuze and Guattari stipulate concerning the plane of immanence is that it cannot be reached by combining healthy and unhealthy bodies without organs. Only healthy bodies without organs function as components of passage linking one body without organs to another to form a plane of immanence. While it is true that Deleuze and Guattari rarely speak in terms of absolutes and they are open to carefully titrated mixtures of healthy and unhealthy they do draw the line at what they describe as cancerous bodies without organs, for which there is no safe dose. They are considered cancerous by Deleuze and Guattari precisely because they are unable to form positive relations with other bodies without organs. Where cancerous bodies without organs predominate the healthier bodies without organs tend to wither so the resulting plane of immanence tends to be cancerous as well. 'This is why the material problem confronting schizoanalysis is knowing whether we have it within our means to make the selection, to distinguish the BwO from its doubles: empty vitreous bodies, cancerous bodies, totalitarian and fascist.'[23] The plane of immanence (consistency) is never a simple aggregate or accumulation of bodies without organs. 'There are things it rejects; the BwO chooses, as a function of the abstract machine that draws it. Even within a BwO (the masochist body, the drugged body, etc.), we must distinguish what can be composed on the plane and what cannot.'[24] This is a delicate process, which as I have said Deleuze and Guattari frame as an art of doses because there are good and bad uses of masochism, of drugs and so on; but for them the real question is one of translation, can the positive effects obtained by unhealthy means – e.g. drugs – be obtained by other means? Hence their therapeutic interest in Henry Miller's notion of getting drunk on pure water.[25] Ultimately, the plane of immanence must be constructed patiently and with care by means of assemblages, which need to be calibrated in such a way as to bring about the desired result:

> This can take place in very different social formations through very different assemblages (perverse, artistic, scientific, mystical, political) with different types of bodies without organs. It is constructed piece by piece, and the places, conditions, and techniques are irreducible to one another. The question, rather, is whether the pieces can fit together, and at what price.[26]

The compatibility of different types of bodies without organs is *the central problematic of Deleuze and Guattari's theory of affect*. This problematic became prominent, at least for me, in the early days of the Covid-19 pandemic (2020–2) when governments everywhere scrambled to respond to a disease threat they didn't fully understand and were woefully underprepared to deal with. It often played out as what appeared to be moral dilemmas, but were in my view indicative of the compound nature of our affect. For example, people who were concerned about the side effects of what to them seemed to be hastily thrown together and essentially untested vaccines found themselves branded as pariahs and lunatics. This, in turn, led many people down a strange political path towards extreme right-wing groups taking radically anti-government positions to the point of declaring themselves exempt from the rules of a government they claimed not to recognize. Meanwhile, many of the same people simply wanted to get on with their lives as they had done before the pandemic and continue to do exactly the same things. They vehemently opposed vaccine mandates and the government's right to impose them, but despite their sabre-rattling rhetoric mostly just wanted to go back to being apolitical and most did when the mandates were abolished. To my mind, the most important lesson from this period was the astonishing rapidity with which political ideas in the form of bodies without organs can combine and create toxic aggregations.

What I am calling a 'toxic aggregation' would be something like an auto-immune condition of the plane of immanence that prevents it from forming properly. Deleuze and Guattari conceive of cancerous bodies without organs, but do not allow for aggregations of these cancerous bodies, but this seems unnecessarily limiting from a conceptual point of view because it leaves us unable to account for the kinds of combinations of bodies without organs one encounters in contemporary forms of fascism – Trump, Bolsonaro, Orban, Modi, Netanyahu and so on. It also opens up an important area of research, namely how and under what conditions can cancerous bodies without organs combine together to form the toxic aggregations like ethnic nationalism? Deleuze and Guattari tend to lump such things together under the general heading of paranoia, but this seems overhasty to me. I think it is more useful to see cancerous bodies without organs as forms capable of attracting desire and altering our way of seeing the world, just as 'regular' bodies without organs do, and ask how these toxic forms are able to combine. To my mind, we saw a living demonstration of some aspects of what's at stake here in the various negative responses to the public health regulations put in place during Covid (mask mandates, lockdowns, vaccines and so on). From a schizoanalytic perspective, what was striking to me was the way a fear molecule could be combined with an anti-government molecule, to take only one example. This was striking because many of the so-called anti-vaxxers were previously fine with vaccines.

In Australia, where public health has long been taken very seriously by the government, vaccinations for a wide range of diseases are a normal part of the life course. As such, there would have been very few, if any, anti-vaxxers who had not at some point been vaccinated. One can of course point the finger at the vast amount of disinformation that circulated – and continues to circulate – on the internet casting doubt on the safety of the vaccines as a reason for people's opposition to being vaccinated. I think, however, there is more to it than that because many anti-vaxxers described themselves as being opposed to vaccine *mandates* rather than vaccines per se, thus making it an issue of control (in precisely Deleuze's sense) rather than public health. Obviously these two standpoints do not cancel each other out, in fact the opposite is true: they resonate and amplify one another. And that is clearly what occurred during the pandemic. The reason I am suggesting this should be seen as an affair of bodies without organs is because it precisely concerns ways of thinking, seeing and feeling, rather than organizational structures (i.e. assemblages). What was interesting in this respect is the fact that most anti-vaxxers continued to believe in a general way in the things they denounced in a specific way. Thus a perhaps healthy scepticism morphed into an irrational fear. They denounced big pharma for profiting from the pandemic – a not unreasonable view – but continued to rely on pharmaceuticals elsewhere in their lives – an irrational view; they denounced the government's right to impose vaccine mandates – a not unreasonable view – but also expected the government to maintain its mandates in other areas of life, such as road rules, minimum wage requirements and so on – an irrational view. Ultimately, I think for many of the anti-vaxxers it was precisely a problem of perception – they could not understand, or make peace with, the fact that their way of seeing the world was so radically out of step with how the majority saw things.

This is why I think the compatibility of different types of bodies without organs is a crucial problem. Indeed, I would say it is *the* crucial problematic for schizoanalysis in general. Unfortunately, Deleuze and Guattari do not offer a fully fleshed-out analytic framework for dealing with this particular problematic. They note its existence but leave it as an open question that can only be assessed via experimentation, which puts it on a level with guesswork. Deleuze's work on Spinoza is no help either because it takes the same approach. It notes that some connections and encounters enhance our capacities, while others diminish them, but again it makes it a matter of experimentation. One may eventually convert the fruit of experiments into knowledge, but it still doesn't give us an analytic framework. I want to approach this problematic in a different way by picking up on the suggestion that Deleuze and Guattari make for thinking about the relation between the plane of immanence and its structural opposite the plane of organization. They suggest that we can treat the plane of immanence and the plane of organization as a formal opposition (dualism by another name). It may seem abusive to describe the plane of immanence and plane of organization as a dualism because Deleuze and Guattari are both so vehemently opposed to dualisms, but as Deleuze acknowledges dualisms are unavoidable. Our strategy, he says, should be to find ways of passing through them in such a way that we undo them from the inside.[27]

In order to find a means of passing through a dualism and undoing it from the inside we first of all need to lay out its coordinates. This means talking about the two planes together: the plane of immanence and the plane of organization. I haven't previously discussed the plane of organization (which also goes by several different names, such as the plane of development and the plane of transcendence), so let me give a brief account of it now. Undoubtedly the most useful way of thinking about the plane of organization is to see it as the point where all the abstract machines intersect (totality).[28] Deleuze and Guattari suggest that the opposition between the two planes can be mapped as the distinction between two abstract poles. Their example is the distinction between the highly organized model of Western music, on the one hand, and the highly fluid model of Eastern music, on the other. One does not cancel out or preclude the other, but neither can they coexist in the same space and time without causing interference:

> The plane of organization is constantly working away at the plane of consistency [i.e. plane of immanence], always trying to plug the lines of flight, stop or interrupt the movements of deterritorialization, weigh them down, restratify them, reconstitute forms and subjects in a dimension of depth. Conversely, the plane of consistency [i.e. plane of immanence] is constantly extricating itself from the plane of organization, causing particles to spin off the strata, scrambling forms by dint of speed or slowness, breaking down functions [i.e. abstract machines] by means of assemblages or microassemblages.[29]

The crucial implication of this example that I want to underscore is that the formal opposition here is not between the plane of immanence as affect and its other, whatever that might be, which is somehow beyond or outside the realm of affect. On the contrary, both poles of this dualism sit within affect. This opens up our understanding of the relation between the plane of immanence and the plane of organization by stipulating that it has two countervailing tendencies that are in a constant state of tension. Our capacity to act is informed as much by forms and functions as it is by metamorphoses and flows – the former gives us effectivity, while the latter gives us resilience. We couldn't plan our day without mobilizing the forms and functions which give it structure, but by the same token we couldn't cope with the various disruptions and derailments our day often brings if we didn't have the capacity to adapt and improvise. If it rains when we expected or wanted sunshine our plans for the day might be ruined, but we can also laugh at our misfortune and still take joy from it.

In this sense, the two planes have a moderating influence on each other. The plane of organization is all that stands between the plane of immanence and a regression into the inhospitable hellscape of the undifferentiated and the slide towards abolition and death. The plane of organization is the most perdurable aspect of affect, that which we call upon to put ourselves back together following periods of (potentially traumatic) dis-individuation, or what Deleuze and Guattari refer to as becoming.[30] In order to exemplify this point, Deleuze and Guattari quote Artaud saying that, on the one hand, the conscious 'knows what is good for it and what is of no value to it: it knows which thoughts and feelings it can receive without danger and with profit, and which are harmful to the exercise of its freedom' (i.e. it is organized and organizing); but, on the other hand, 'there is in human existence another plane, obscure and formless, where consciousness has not entered, and, which surrounds it like an unilluminated extension or menace, as the case may be. And which itself gives off adventurous sensations, perceptions. These are the shameless fantasies which affect an unhealthy consciousness.'[31] Here Artaud articulates perfectly the difference between the plane of organization and the plane of immanence as the difference between a form of sensing that gives rise to recognition and a form of sensing that does not: the first form of sensing is subject to calculations and judgements about good and bad, true and false, while the latter form is not – it can only be felt, and in being felt can only be felt as affections ('adventurous sensations, perceptions'). How we map this tension between the opposing tendencies of the two planes is the key to the analytic framework I want to establish here.

Each plane has its own powers. While the powers are distinct they are also mutually presupposed: the plane of immanence cannot function in the absence of the plane of organization, and vice versa. In this sense, one is encasted in the other as its condition of possibility. The plane of organization – which consists of interlinked abstract machines and manifests as strata – has a diagrammatic power: it manifests in several different ways, as differences, as functions, as the distinction between signifier and signified. By contrast, the plane of immanence has a destratifying power: it too manifests in several different ways, as movement, transformation, metamorphosis and so on. Borges's account of the *Celestial Emporium of Benevolent Knowledge* in the essay 'The Analytic Language of John Wilkins' which so amused and inspired Foucault is a perfect illustration of what is at stake:

This passage quotes a 'certain Chinese encyclopedia' in which it is written that 'animals are divided into: (a) belonging to the Emperor, (b) embalmed, (c) tame, (d) sucking pigs, (e) sirens, (f) fabulous, (g) stray dogs, (h) included in the present classification, (i) frenzied, (j) innumerable, (k) drawn with a very fine camel hair brush, (l) *et cetera*, (m) having just broken the water pitcher, (n) that from a long way off look like flies'.[32]

Foucault argues that this marvellous fable makes one thing very apparent, namely the limited nature of our own system of thought (plane of organization) such that we find it impossible to think *that* (plane of immanence). But, he goes on to ask, which aspect of this table is impossible to think? What kind of impossibility is it? The problem isn't the specific elements themselves, regardless of how strange they might seem, because the table carefully separates them out, thus avoiding the 'possibility of dangerous mixtures'.[33] The fabulous nature of some of the categories isn't a problem because they are explicitly designated as such. Although the lack of a gap separating categories like 'embalmed' and 'tame' is troubling, as is their juxtaposition, that isn't the real problem either. Neither is the strange propinquity of things that do not seem to belong together decisive, such as one finds in Lautréamont's famous definition of beauty (the chance meeting of an umbrella and sewing-machine on an operating table), because however improbable such an event is it is not impossible. What is actually impossible, he argues, is not their propinquity, but the common ground on which such a propinquity would be possible. *That* it is what we cannot think. 'Where else could they be juxtaposed except in the non-place of language? Yet, though language can spread before them before us. It can only do so in an unthinkable space.'[34] Foucault concludes that the absurdity of this table 'destroys the *and* of the enumeration by making impossible the *in* where the things enumerated would be divided up'.[35]

But what really makes him uneasy, he realizes, is the fact that however startling this strange taxonomy may be it is still preferable to a situation in which the categories themselves, despite their strangeness, lose their identity altogether and we can longer distinguish between sirens and sucking pigs. This is exactly how the plane of immanence and plane of organization relate to one another: the plane of immanence is the space *in* which the enumerations of the plane of organization – i.e. 'and, and, and' – is possible. Schizophrenia, as Deleuze and Guattari grasp it, can be understood in terms of a radical separation between the two planes, such that the 'laws' that typically apply to what is and what is not thinkable in a given moment are set aside. In *Anti-Oedipus* they describe it as an instance of an inclusive disjunction, which is to say a form of connection, or sequence, in which the law of non-contradiction no longer applies. They give two examples to illustrate this point, both of which are given as instances of becoming at work. They provoke essentially the same reaction Foucault had to the *Celestial Emporium of Benevolent Knowledge*, namely the stark impossibility of thinking *that*. The first is from Beckett's *Molloy*: 'It is midnight. The rain is beating on the windows. It was not midnight. It was not raining.' And the second is taken from Nijinsky's diary: 'I am God I was not God I am a clown of God; I am Apis. I am an Egyptian. I am a red Indian. I am a Negro. I am a Chinaman. I am a Japanese. I am a foreigner, a stranger. I am a sea bird. I am a land bird. I am the tree of Tolstoy. I am the roots of Tolstoy ... I am a husband and wife in one. I love my wife. I love my husband.'[36] Our sense of the sheer impossibility of thinking like this is the feeling we get, which Deleuze and Guattari refer to as becoming, when the plane of immanence breaks with the plane of organization.

The Framework

The two planes taken together map thinkability, if you will, in terms of a single problem: What 'laws' govern the combination of things? Foucault's astonishment regarding the *Celestial Emporium of Benevolent Knowledge* derives from the fact that there does not appear to be any discernible law shaping the structure of the classification table. Put simply, there is no way of knowing what could and could not be included in the table. It is, as he says, ungrounded, and in that sense appears mad. Deleuze and Guattari's fascination with Artaud, Beckett, Nijinsky and others is similarly concerned with the apparent ungroundedness of their utterances, which do not even seem to respect the law of non-contradiction ('I am God I was not God'). Indeed, one of the reasons Deleuze wanted to meet Guattari was precisely to learn more about schizophrenic utterances, which he had become interested in while writing about the problem of nonsense in *The Logic of Sense*. Schizophrenic utterances differ from nonsense because they do not so much concern impossible objects or impossible situations, such as one finds in Lewis Carroll, which are intended to be humorous, but something much more complex and difficult to pin down, namely the feeling of an unwilled and perhaps even unwanted transformation. Deleuze and Guattari's key example is Freud's patient the Wolf-Man who, on their description, simultaneously felt like he was becoming a wolf and knew that he wasn't actually about to turn into a wolf. They classify this feeling as 'becoming'. I will discuss this at greater length in Chapter 4. For now, suffice it to note that it is very different from what Lewis Carroll's Alice experiences. Despite all the absurdities Alice encounters – talking rabbits in top hats, talking playing cards and so on – she never ceases to feel like herself.

In absurdity the plane of immanence and the plane of organization remain attached to one another, the one limiting the development of the other. Alice remains a fixed point of view (plane of organization) on the unfolding events (plane of immanence). No matter how absurd things get on the plane of immanence, her perspective on them remains organized, which among other things means she can distinguish between possible and impossible, logical and illogical, and so on. She does not change in herself even as her circumstances undergo dramatic transformations. At times she even finds this disappointing, as in the episode when she eats cake. 'Alice had got so much into the way of expecting nothing but out-of-the-way things to happen, that it seemed quite dull and stupid for life to go on in the common way.'[37] But even the absurd things she encounters she encounters in an ordinary way – she gets frustrated, to be sure, but she never feels as though she is no longer herself.

There is no becoming in Carroll (here one must observe that the becoming articulated in *The Logic of Sense* is not the same as that articulated in *A Thousand Plateaus*). By contrast, in H. P. Lovecraft, becoming is the ground bass of everything he writes. In one of his masterpieces, H. P. Lovecraft recounts the story of Carter, who feels his 'self' reel and who experiences a fear worse than that of annihilation. 'Carters of forms both human and non-human, vertebrate and invertebrate, conscious and mindless, animal and vegetable. And more, there were Carters having nothing in common with earthly life but moving outrageously amidst backgrounds of other planets and systems and galaxies and cosmic continua . . .'[38] As Carter merges with the cosmos he loses all sense of himself as a separate being, and that is for him 'the nameless summit of agony and dread'.[39] Becoming is a process of desubjectification whereby the subject 'I' ceases to be a bounded entity – e.g. the ego – with a defined relation to an outside and becomes instead an unbounded entity that knows a thousand different names ('I am God I was not God').[40] These names have no meanings in themselves, they simply mark out the borders of zones of intensity which the schizo has moved through and derived a certain surplus value from. In Lovecraft, the plane of immanence sets itself free from the constraints of the plane of organization and everything slides towards the hellscape of abolition and death.

The two planes do not by themselves provide us with an analytic framework, which is why Deleuze and Guattari invented two other concepts that map the 'structure', if you will, of the plane of immanence and the plane of organization: the arborescent and the rhizomatic. Here it will be helpful, I think, to take the risk of rewriting these terms into a different conceptual language, one that I am confident was in fact their starting point in any case.[41] So it is less a case of rewriting than it is a case of scratching away the paint to see what was there originally. The arborescent takes its name from trees, though the trees they have in mind are the kind one finds in linguistic textbooks tracing the lineage of particular words rather than the botanical variety.[42] The idea that it refers to actual trees is reinforced by the notion of the rhizomatic which is in fact botanical in origin but, as I have argued elsewhere, no amount of studying plant biology will ever yield much insight into the nature of this concept. Hence the usefulness of rewriting these terms. The point of origin for both terms is in fact structural linguistics. This may seem like heresy on my part, but it's worth bearing in mind that Deleuze and Guattari wrote their books in the heyday of structuralism. Deleuze's essay 'How do we recognize structuralism' makes it clear he was both very familiar with structuralism and not unsympathetic to it without in any way identifying with it.[43] So one shouldn't be surprised to find traces of it in their work, albeit heavily reworked. This does not mean anything as facile as they were closet structuralists; rather, it simply means they repurposed some structuralist terms and ideas that they found useful.

The arborescent, which maps the structure of the plane of organization, whose essential mode is that of the diagram, corresponds to what in structural linguistics is known as the diachronic. By contrast, the rhizomatic, which maps the structure of plane of immanence, corresponds to the synchronic. The terms 'synchronic' and 'diachronic' are usually taken to mean, 'in a sort of vulgar sense', as Jameson puts it, 'the present and historical succession', but, as he says, this is reductive.[44] Jameson notes that the term 'diachronic' seems to have first of all been used in geology by Charles Lyell, a contemporary of Charles Darwin, who used it to envisage deep historical time, going against the prevailing biblical view that the earth was merely a few thousand years old. His argument, which influenced Darwin's evolution of the species hypothesis, is that everything we see around us today is the product of determinate actions going back millions of years. In short, the present is explained by the past.

Here it is important to note that although Deleuze and Guattari's notion of strata is derived from geological thinking of precisely this variety (as I have previously shown) they are in fact synchronic not diachronic. Jean-Baptiste Fressoz's polemic against the notion of the 'energy transition' *More and More and More* offers a startling illustration of this point. As he argues, the notion of 'energy transition' embraced by many energy historians naturalizes the empirically false idea that over time wood has been exchanged for coal as a primary energy source and in turn coal has been exchanged for oil and now if we all try hard enough oil can be exchanged for renewables. Climate change deniers use this to claim that coal saved forests and whales from extinction by offering an alternative higher density energy source. This is a diachronic view of strata which holds that each new energy source serves as a precursor to the next which at the moment of transition becomes obsolete. However, as Fressoz demonstrates, there has never been an energy transition, if by that one means one energy source is swapped for another. Instead, what has happened is that each new energy source has led to an increase in the use of the 'old' energy source. Far more wood is burned for energy today than at any other point in history. Not only that, wood remains an essential resource for mining – timber is used in coal mines for tunnel stays, among other things – so much so that even if were true that the burning of coal was supplanting the burning of wood for energy trees would still be under enormous pressure.[45] Wood, coal, oil and gas can be thought of as strata because they are distinct in themselves and there are relations of dependency between them, but one cannot treat them as determining one another. There is no determinate path from windmills to steam engines and the latter did not render the former obsolete. The relation between the strata is instead one of resonance and amplification, not just of the total amount of energy consumed, but of the idea that energy consumption is a 'normal', non-negotiable part of everyday life. It is the task of the abstract machine – or, rather, the plane of organization – to hold these diverse strata together by mobilizing assemblages capable of interacting with one another despite their differences.

In order to better understand this point it is useful to think about how destratification would work in this context. The notion of 'energy transition' makes it seem that the so-called transitions between wood, coal, oil and gas and so on are all forms of destratification whereby one stratum gives way to another. But this is not only factually erroneous, as we've seen, it is also conceptually weak because it misses the fact that the energy consumption continues to increase irrespective of the energy source. That is to say, it forgets to ask what the strata are for: What effect do they produce? Viewed from that perspective, from the perspective of energy production and consumption, destratification would have to take the form of a disruption of the energy consumption continuum. The shift to so-called renewable energy sources does not meet this standard and in fact it is demonstrably the case that in many instances the allegedly 'greener' option isn't that green after all. For example, the electric car is manufactured using coal – thermal and metallurgical – and its component parts and base materials as well as the finished product are transported on oil-burning ships, and as Trump happily announced in many cases the electricity that powers them comes from coal-burning power stations. It may be that the electric car is far more efficient in its use of energy than fossil fuel vehicles, but it is nevertheless anything but a transition from non-renewable to renewable energy. It is, rather, yet another way of consuming energy that will ultimately lead to a net increase in our energy consumption. The language of sustainability used in this context conceals in plain sight what is actually at stake: the electric vehicle is simply a means of sustaining a high energy consumption lifestyle in the guise of an allegedly 'greener' option. As such, it cannot be considered a form of destratification. Actual destratification would take the form of a conscious refusal of the high energy consumption lifestyle (which we can probably add to the list of what we'd find more difficult to imagine than the end of the world).[46]

One paradoxical effect of the diachronic approach is that we can never go back far enough in our search for an explanation of the genesis of a contemporary event. The French historian Fernand Braudel is probably the one who took this idea the most to heart in his expansive histories of the Mediterranean region.[47] This notion of geological time underpins Deleuze and Guattari's concept of strata, as I have explained elsewhere, but their take on deep time is far more dynamic than Lyell's in that they theorize processes of stratification and destratification. This amounts to saying that it is possible for certain aspects of the past to cease to have an influence on the present and somehow sputter out like a decommissioned branch line. In this regard if we need to map their concepts of stratification and destratification against an actual model of evolution it would probably be closest to Stephen Jay Gould's so-called punctuated equilibrium model, which – like Deleuze and Guattari – emphasizes the part contingency has to play in the development of forms. Contingency disrupts the order of things in such a way that the laws of development can no longer be called upon to explain every aspect of the present. His key demonstration of this point, as I have mentioned before, is the Burgess shale:

> With so many Burgess possibilities of apparently equivalent anatomical promise – over twenty arthropod designs later decimated to four survivors, perhaps fifteen or more unique anatomies available for recruitment as major branches, or phyla, of life's tree – our modern pattern of anatomical disparity is thrown into the lap of contingency. The modern order was not guaranteed by basic laws (natural selection, mechanical superiority in anatomical design), or even by lower-level generalities of ecology or evolutionary theory. The modern order is largely a product of contingency.[48]

The past does not always explain the present; history does not always unfold in a linear, or path-dependent manner, with one event leading mechanically to another. Sometimes history's lines of descent reach an abrupt end as Gould argues is the case with the fossilised fauna from the Cambrian period found in the Burgess shale. History must also account for these kinds of disruptions that throw all the basic laws to the wind and initiate changes which can only be thought of as leaps. Once those leaps have occurred, a new line of descent may be initiated, but the crucial point is it cannot be connected directly to what came before. The past may prepare the ground for the future, but it does not always explain it. In these circumstances, the line of descent becomes a zigzag, or as Deleuze and Guattari call it, transversal. Like Gould, they think evolutionary schemas need to allow for sudden shifts and leaps that do not follow a strict line of descent. In doing so, 'they would no longer follow models of arborescent descent going from the least to the most differentiated, but instead a rhizome operating immediately in the heterogeneous and jumping from one already differentiated line to another'.[49]

It was in fact the so-called father of structuralism who first began to dispute the relevance of the diachronic approach to the history of languages, despite having written one of the great works on the subject himself. In a much-quoted letter, Saussure wrote: 'I'm coming to think that nothing we're doing in linguistics right now has any meaning and is of any value.'[50] This is because the charts created by Franz Bopp, the Grimm brothers (of fairy-tale fame) and others, tracing the multitude of small transformations that lead us from a hypothesized original language (Indo-European) down through the centuries to the current state of differentiation between modern European languages, tell us very little about contemporary language use. It can explain how one word can over time change in sound, structure and meaning, but it cannot explain why that word is used in a particular context. For example, the English word 'ship' is derived from Old English *scip* (noun), late Old English *scipian* (verb), which is originally of Germanic origin and is related to Dutch *schip* and German *Schiff*. This explains why we have this word in English and why it sounds the way it does. But it does not explain why we choose to call machines capable of interstellar flight 'spaceships'. We can of course surmise why this word was chosen, because space craft are comparable in several respects to ocean-going vessels, but there is no law of linguistic derivation that applies. For that reason, Saussure felt it was necessary to approach language in a different way. Instead of following lines of descent, whereby one term gives rise to the next term, he started to look at language as a system that operates in the present. His great insight was to realize that insofar as the present of language is concerned, it literally doesn't matter where words come from, or how they are derived, including the most microscopic parts of words, all that matters is that they are differentiated from one another. This gives rise to the central principle of structuralism as we know it: 'In language there are only differences without positive terms.'[51] In other words it doesn't matter how or why we say 'ship' in English, what matters is that we can distinguish it from 'shit'.

Here, then, we have the formal difference between the arborescent schema of the plane of organization and the rhizomatic schema of the plane of immanence: the first presupposes lines of derivation from one positive term to another – these may be precipitated by, or disrupted by, clean breaks, but this simply starts or restarts the process of derivation; the second presupposes lines of difference without positive terms – these can and do give rise to clean breaks, too, that then set in motion arborescent lines, but their main function, if you will, is to segment the present, and generate systems of difference. The first has extension, but the second lacks it – the plane of immanence consists solely of intensities.

Affect as a psychical agency consists of these two planes and their underlying schemas operating in tandem, each acting as a limit on the other, one by closing doors and imposing forms and functions and the other by opening doors and undoing forms and functions. The relative state of the doors opened versus doors closed determines whether and how we can meet the day: too closed and we feel like we are crushed under a heavy weight, too open and we feel like we're drowning in an open sea.

Assemblages are our psychical means of steering a course between the two undesirable situations. The assemblage sits 'between' these two planes: it actualizes the 'diagram' of the plane of organization and it generates and sustains the plane of immanence. The plane that works for me is the one that not only keeps my head above water but also enables me to swim with the current. Understanding that affect has both a diachronic and synchronic dimension amounts to realizing that some aspects of its composition are a product of our history and our situation and can therefore be derived (plane of organization), but other aspects are not attributable to our history and our situation and must therefore be understood in terms of the flows it unleashes and sustains (plane of immanence).

4 AFFECT AND BECOMING

Of course, new concepts must relate to our problems, to our history, and, above all, to our becomings.[1]

One of the reasons I wanted to take the risk, as it were, of attempting to rewrite Deleuze and Guattari's concepts in a different conceptual language – one that they themselves rewrote in order to end up where they did, I hasten to add – is that it gives us a more formal framework into which all of their concepts can then be placed. This, in turn, helps to put us onto the path of using their concepts in a rigorously analytical rather than merely adjectival way. This is not to suggest that Deleuze and Guattari's work is just structural linguistics in disguise, it is obviously not that. But the diachronic and synchronic binary is useful because it helps to frame one of the key problems they address in their work: How can we understand schizophrenic utterances? They reject Freud's assumption that schizophrenic utterances can be understood in the same way as non-schizophrenic utterances of the Oedipal variety. Their meaning cannot be derived by tracing everything back to a 'primal scene' – sometimes the wolf is just a wolf and not an avatar of the father. They also reject the idea that schizophrenic utterances are entirely without meaning, that they are simply the indecipherable ravings of benighted individuals. In this sense it is perfectly accurate to think of the plane of immanence on which the schizophrenic utterances are grounded as synchronic because, as Jameson reminds us, in linguistics synchronic does not merely mean 'in the present' it also implies that there is a system. And that is precisely how Deleuze and Guattari approach schizophrenic utterances: as a system. This system has 'rules', or at least observable regularities (as Foucault puts it), that Deleuze and Guattari attempt to map with their concept of becoming. We can begin to get a handle on how becoming works by understanding that in a formal sense it is precisely a system of 'differences without positive terms'. In contrast to psychoanalysis's understanding of hysterical utterances, schizoanalysis does not recognize any privileged terms – daddy, mummy, me and so on are all treated as bands of intensity to move through with no more or less significance than any other term.

Psychoanalysis, much like philology from which it drew a great deal of inspiration, always assumes that the present situation can only be explained with reference to history, which it treats as an arborescent line of descent leading from a primal scene to the present. Freud's interpretation of the Wolf-Man's dream of five wolves in a tree outside his bedroom window is exemplary in this regard. As Deleuze and Guattari complain, he never once considers that the wolves might be meaningful in themselves. 'The Wolf-Man keeps howling: Six wolves! Seven Wolves! Freud says, How's that? Goats, you say? How interesting. Take away the goats and all you have left is a wolf, so it's your father.'[2] By contrast, schizoanalysis, much like structural linguistics from which it drew a great deal of inspiration, treats the present situation as a meaningful system in and of itself which does not require reference to an external system in order to be understood. On their reading of the Wolf-Man's dream the wolves are not treated as representatives of an Oedipal system that merely requires minimal decoding to see, but rather as meaningful in themselves, though not necessarily for themselves. The one thing their reading of the Wolf-Man wants to avoid at all costs is a return to an arborescent model, so although they start by considering the wolves from a representative point of view, focusing on the specific characteristics of wolves and their reception in culture, they do not end there. Ultimately, the wolves are deemed to be merely zones of intensity, as Deleuze and Guattari put it, that the schizophrenic moves through on their way somewhere else. Becoming is not a transformation of one form into another – a man into a wolf, let's say – it is the feeling that one no longer is what one was and as such one can therefore be either anything or nothing.

Becoming as a process can be understood in a formal way as that which follows the scission between the plane of immanence and the plane of organization, i.e. between the synchronic and the diachronic, such that our interpretation of it can no longer even be called 'interpretation' because it is impossible to derive its meaning from a pre-existing assemblage such as the Oedipal complex. Becoming spawns its own assemblages and if we want to try to understand them then we need to approach them in an immanent manner and start by asking: How do they work? This can in turn be broken down into a series of even more precisely targeted questions: What type of body without organs do they give rise to? (i.e. what new ways of thinking, seeing and feeling do they engender?) Is it capable of connecting to a plane of immanence? What type of abstract machine undergirds them? What are their lines of flight from their abstract machines? And so on. The problem at issue is essentially hermeneutic in nature (as much of Freud's work is) because it poses the question of how to read, decipher and understand a class of symptomal behaviour Deleuze and Guattari classify as 'becoming-animal'. The concept of becoming is clearly intended to render visible a very particular kind of experience – which I will call 'the strange imperative' – and at the same time distinguish it from all other types of experience, particularly those identified and enumerated by psychoanalysis (which Jameson usefully refers to as the 'psychopathologies of the ego').[3] But, it also desperately wants to avoid the fate of reifying the thing it names and thereby turning it into something concrete that we think we can know. In this sense, becoming should always be understood to stand in opposition to emotion, or what Jameson more precisely calls 'named emotions', because what it seeks to name and bring into the light is a set of experiences that have hitherto escaped detection, or else – more usually – have been written off as mad, fantastical, horrific and so on.

Every time we feel we are getting a handle on becoming in a concrete sense we need to take a step back and ask ourselves if we are being abstract enough. For instance, the Wolf-Man's fascination with wolves should not be confused with the named emotion fear, in either its Freudian or Heideggerian senses of being a form of anxiety induced by an actual object. Although Deleuze and Guattari say that becoming-animal does not take place 'without a fascination for the pack', that should not be taken to mean that this fascination is in some way causal. In contrast to fear, it is not the sight of wolves, as fearsome objects external to the subject, that triggers a becoming-animal.[4] It would be truer to say that the Wolf-Man's fascination is itself a sign that he has entered a state of becoming: he is fascinated *because* of his becoming-animal, not the other way round. Becoming is something that happens to us, as though a switch inside our heads has been flicked. 'It is because the hero of *Focus*, the average American, needs glasses that give his nose a vaguely Semitic air, it is "because of the glasses" that he is thrown into [*précipité*] this strange adventure of the becoming-Jewish of the non-Jew.'[5] Deleuze and Guattari

go onto say anything at all can precipitate this change of mental gears –
Massumi translates *précipité* as 'thrown into', but this seems unnecessarily
Heideggerian and misleading to the extent that it implies that in becoming
one enters 'another world', when in actual fact what happens is one begins
to see and experience 'this world' very differently.[6] In the framework I
am suggesting here, one can say it propels one into a purely synchronic
system of meanings.

One may wonder why Deleuze and Guattari use such a strange
locution as 'becoming', which is actually a misnomer since there is no
suggestion that anyone is going to transmogrify. My sense is they felt
compelled to go in this direction because of the inadequacy of the word
'like' for capturing and expressing this particular feeling of transformation.
As Deleuze and Guattari say, if we treat 'like' as the index of a metaphor
or analogy, then we miss what is essential in becoming.[7] 'Like' changes its
meaning, according to Deleuze and Guattari, depending on whether it
is used in a molar or molecular sense. In the molar mode, which is its
traditional sense, it creates a structure of analogy – a man can chew on
iron in the same way a dog chews on a bone, but this does not initiate a
process of becoming-animal because it is not driven by a felt need
for transformation.[8] When 'like' is used in the molecular mode it refers
to something else entirely. Its starting position is very different. Instead
of beginning with two solid entities who happen to act in the same way
(a man chewing an iron bar and a dog chewing a bone), the molecular
'like' starts from the position that these solid entities are actually
composed of a multiplicity of differential traits that are, or can be made
to become, combinable in such a way as to be able to create new forms.
Computer graphics allow us to envisage what Deleuze and Guattari are
trying to say here quite easily (it could be done on a smartphone). If we
start with the images of a man and a dog and then use the zoom function
to expand the images in such a way that the individual pixels in each
image become less and less integrated with one another and we stop
seeing a man and a dog and instead see colours, shapes, textures and so
on to the point where the differences between the man and the dog are no
longer discernible, then we have a visual rendering of becoming. 'You
become animal only molecularly. You do not become a barking molar
dog, but by barking, if it is done with enough feeling, with enough
necessity and composition, you emit a molecular dog.'[9] It is a question of
composition rather than resemblance (even when the end result appears
the same).

This is the first rule of becoming: *becoming is always double*. 'Becoming is always double, that which one becomes becomes no less than the one that becomes – block is formed, essentially mobile, never in equilibrium.'[10] This rule is fundamental to both the 'psychological' cases we'll be considering here and what might be termed Deleuze and Guattari's aesthetics. Indeed, I would go so far as to say that the latter shapes the former because it is there that one finds a theory of composition, which is encapsulated in the following proposition: 'No art is imitative, no art can be imitative or figurative.'[11] An artist may think they are representing a bird, Deleuze and Guattari say, but this is in fact a self-deception because executing a likeness is only possible to the degree that the bird itself can become something else, namely a series of lines, brushstrokes, colours and so on. But even before the painter can get to the stage of putting paint on a canvas they have to have already begun to see the bird as a multiplicity of differential traits – the sharpness of the talons, the shininess of the plumage, the curvature of the beak and so on. This is why the likeness of a bird can be produced with just a few lines as Picasso famously did with his lithograph now known as the *Dove of Peace* (1961), or with blocks of colour in a contorted shape as he did with *Bird on a Tree* (1928). 'If resemblance haunts the work of art, it is because sensation refers only to its material: it is the percept or affect of the material, the *smile* of the oil, the *gesture* of fired clay, the *thrust* of metal, the *crouch* of Romanesque stone, the *ascent* of Gothic stone.'[12] Smile, gesture, thrust, crouch and ascent are all differential traits in the sense that they give life to the work of art by bringing it into relation with these deterritorialized capacities of living creatures.

Something in This World *Forces* Us To Think

For the conceptual origin of the concept of becoming as that which *precipitates* a 'crisis' in one's sense of who one is we need to once again return to *Difference and Repetition* and the passage we discussed in Chapter 2. Deleuze writes: 'Something in this world *forces* us to think. This something is an object not of recognition but of a fundamental encounter [. . .] It may be grasped in a range of affective tones: wonder, love, hatred, suffering. In whichever tone, its primary characteristic is that it can only be sensed.'[13] This something is not an object of recognition because, as

Deleuze explains, in recognition the sensible 'bears directly upon the senses in an object which can be recalled, imagined, or conceived.'[14] The sensible object 'presupposes the exercise of the senses and the exercise of the other faculties in a common sense.'[15] By contrast, the object of the encounter ('this something that forces us to think') gives rise to its own form of sensibility, which Deleuze and Guattari refer to as becoming. The essential characteristic of this particular form of sensibility is that it is constituted as an encounter with its own limit, its own empirical impossibility: something that can be sensed but cannot be recognized is empirically impossible, yet must happen all the time, or we wouldn't think, dream or create art. The impossible is possible in dreams, and in art – think of Surrealism – precisely because the objects encountered are sensed without being recognized they give rise to effects and feelings, but not recognition. 'It is not the gods which we encounter: even hidden, the gods are only the forms of recognition. What we encounter are the demons, the sign-bearers: powers of the leap, the interval, the intensive and the instant; powers which only cover difference with more difference.'[16]

This is what Kant demonstrated with the concept of the sublime, according to Deleuze – in exceeding what can be recognized, the sublime can only be sensed, and that is precisely its power, because by virtue of this fact it exerts a form of violence on the faculties that forces us to think.[17] The mountain range, the forest, the ocean, all of nature's majesties, exceed the capacity of our senses to recognize them fully, which would perhaps manifest as the ability to find words adequate to the feeling they induce, so they leave us speechless and in awe, which is why they emblematize the sublime for Kant.[18] This feeling, though, is easily destroyed, all one has to do is think of these things – the mountain range, forest and ocean – in terms of their potential economic value, as the extractive industries do, then they are reduced to the logistical challenges they pose and their poetic potential is lost. The mountain is thinkable as a certain amount of coal or iron ore to be extracted and transported elsewhere, but not as something timeless and mysterious, something that pre-dates human presence and if not for our greed would still be around after we're gone. Art, on this view of things, can be thought of as the ongoing attempt to generate new forms of 'this something that forces us to think' in the face of the many ways by which thought is captured and forestalled by interest. But, as Deleuze cautions, everyone 'knows that, if an art necessarily imposed the shock or vibration, the world would have changed long ago, and men [*sic*] would have been thinking for a long time.'[19] As such, the pretensions of great auteurs make us smile, Deleuze says.

At stake here is the possibility of thinking itself, a problematic Deleuze associates with schizophrenia.[20] What we are capable of thinking at any given moment is a function of affect, which means that affect is a dimension of thought itself. 'Nothing is more exemplary in this respect,' he says, 'than the exchange of letters between Jacques Rivière and Antonin Artaud.'[21] For Rivière the problem is framed in terms of the difficulty one may have in thinking about a particular topic, due to a poor method of approach, lack of application, lack of training or inadequate background knowledge. These are all problems that can be overcome, such that we can even take pleasure in overcoming these types of obstacles because they allow us to see ourselves in a superior light. We've done the work and earned the reward of self-affirmation. Is there anything more gratifying than conquering a maths problem, or a complex passage of philosophy, and feeling the warm glow of understanding as recognition sinks in? For Artaud, though, the problem is elsewhere. 'Artaud said that the problem (for him) was not to orient his thought, or to perfect the expression of what he thought, or to acquire application and method or to perfect his poems, but simply to manage to think something.'[22] This is not just a matter of doing the work and overcoming obstacles. Something else is going on. For Artaud the difficulty of thinking something isn't a state of affairs that can be rectified by the application of 'better' technique, it is a fault – if that's the right word – in the structure of thought itself, meaning that within the structure of what we call thinking there is the ever-present possibility of non-thinking, of a form of thinking that fails to start. 'To think is to create – there is no other creation – but to create is first of all to engender "thinking" in thought.'[23] This 'thinking' which is 'creating' is becoming because it stems from a modulation *in the structure of our affect.*

This power of thinking/creating is sometimes called chaos, but as Deleuze and Guattari explain, chaos is not defined by the absence of determination as is commonly supposed, but rather the infinite speed with which new determinations appear and disappear.[24] For Deleuze and Guattari the power of creation belongs to philosophy *by right.* Here one can see the stark and literally absolute difference between Deleuze and Badiou (perhaps explaining why Deleuze broke off their correspondence), because this means that for Deleuze truth is philosophy's creation, whereas for Badiou truth is philosophy's creator. 'The relationship of thought to truth in the ambiguities of infinite movement has never been a simple, let alone constant, matter. That is why it is pointless to rely on such a relationship to define philosophy.'[25] If, as Nietzsche has shown, there is no 'will to truth', then that is because 'thought constitutes a simple "possibility" of thinking without yet defining a thinker "capable" of it and able to say "I".'[26] The possibility of thought is not, by itself, a guarantee that thought has or will take place, much less that it can or will give rise to philosophy. The simple possibility of thought is rooted in a profound incapacity to think that for Deleuze and Guattari defines the general condition of thought itself and in their view can only be remedied by 'the "violence" of an infinite movement' which is what they ultimately mean by becoming.[27]

The something that forces us to think – i.e. that which precipitates becoming – begins as an irresistible and irrepressible *I feel* that in certain situations can manifest as a compulsion to do, think, see or feel something that takes us outside of ourselves in such a way that we begin to doubt the continued existence of our self. We enter a state Deleuze and Guattari refer to as becoming. For instance, the 'German preromantic Karl Philipp Moritz feels responsible not for the calves that die but before the calves that die and give him the incredible feeling of an unknown Nature – *affect*. For the affect is not a personal feeling, nor is it a characteristic; it is the effectuation of a power of the pack that throws the self into upheaval and makes it reel'.[28] Such feelings, they go onto say, 'uproot one from humanity, if only for an instant, making one scrape at one's bread like a rodent or giving one the yellow eyes of a feline'.[29] Along the same lines, Hofmannsthal's Lord Chandos 'becomes fascinated with a "people" of dying rats, and it is in him, through him, in the interstices of his disrupted self that the "soul of the animal bares its teeth at monstrous fate": not pity, but *unnatural participation*. Then a *strange imperative* wells up in him: either stop writing, or write like a rat . . .'[30] As is clear from this handful of examples, affect is not simply a capacity to affect and to be affected, it is a much more powerful kick in the pants than that, as Lacan says somewhere about the notion of the drive. Becoming is affect – which is to say, desire – in its 'pure', 'free' or 'unbound' state, i.e. free from the limiting effects of the plane of organization:

> There is a schizophrenic experience of intensive quantities in their pure state, to a point that is almost unbearable – a celibate misery and glory experienced to the fullest, like a cry suspended between life and death,

an intense feeling of transition, states of pure naked intensity stripped of all shape and form. These are often described as hallucinations and delirium, but the basic phenomenon of hallucination (*I see*, *I hear*) and the basic phenomenon of delirium (*I think*) presuppose an *I feel* at an even deeper level, which gives hallucinations their object and thought delirium its content – an 'I feel that I am becoming a woman', 'that I am becoming a god', and so on, which is neither delirious nor hallucinatory, but will project the hallucination or internalize the delirium.[31]

It is this 'I feel', this 'intense feeling of transition', which consists in the combination and circulation of elements of our affect understood as a plane of immanence that has broken free from the plane of organization, that becoming conceptualizes. It is this 'I feel' that schizoanalysis as a whole is dedicated to trying to understand and articulate as a functional logic and not an ineffable falling apart. Here we see an essential premise of Deleuze and Guattari's project: 'Delirium and hallucination are secondary in relation to the *really primary emotion*, which in the beginning only experiences intensities, becomings, transitions.'[32] This state of being is unimaginable in the absence of the concept of the body without organs and the plane of immanence. It is only on the body without organs that the impossible transitions implied by becoming-animal, becoming-woman and so on are possible.

We are first introduced to the concept of becoming in the opening pages of *A Thousand Plateaus*, but it isn't until the second chapter which revisits Freud's famous case history of the Wolf-Man that we begin to get a sense of what this concept is really about. It's worth spending some time on the Wolf-Man chapter because Deleuze and Guattari use it as foil to expose what might be termed the structural limits of psychoanalysis and at the same open up a new area of investigation that calls for a new hermeneutic model. Here one can but agree with Jameson that Deleuze and Guattari's anti-interpretation stance 'amounts less to a wholesale nullification of all interpretive activity than to a demand for the construction of some new and more adequate, immanent or antitranscendent hermeneutic model'.[33] It is the basic task of the chapter on the Wolf-Man to demonstrate why this 'more adequate hermeneutic model' is in fact required. The case against Freud is easily made because as Deleuze and Guattari's gleeful satirizing makes clear psychoanalysis is not well-equipped to deal with schizophrenia. Freud acknowledged as much, blaming lack of access to schizophrenic patients as the reason he had not developed an adequate account of schizophrenia's aetiology. It is doubtful, however, that even with greater opportunity to engage with schizophrenic patients he would have been willing to give up on the Oedipal complex as a universal truth of all human behaviour. Deleuze and Guattari do not dispute the existence of the Oedipal complex, but they do dispute its universality. And in the case of schizophrenic patients, they say it has no place at all.

The Wolf-Man and the Strange Imperative

Freud's 1915 essay 'The Unconscious' is Deleuze and Guattari's point of departure for their revisionary account of the Wolf-Man's case history. They credit Freud with making 'an important clinical discovery' in identifying the difference in 'style', as they put it, 'between neurosis and psychosis'.[34] But then they accuse him of effectively turning his back on his own discovery by finding increasingly elaborate and ingenious ways of making psychosis look the same as neurosis after all. The crucial distinction between neurosis and psychosis, according to Deleuze and Guattari's account of Freud, resides in the fact that while neurotics are 'capable of making a global comparison between a sock and a vagina, a scar and castration' it would never occur to them 'to grasp the skin erotically as a multiplicity of pores, little spots, little scars or black holes, or to grasp the sock erotically as a multiplicity of stitches'.[35] This, Deleuze and Guattari say, is illustrated in the work of Salvador Dali – when he speaks about the rhinoceros horn he remains firmly in the realm of neurosis, but 'when he starts comparing goosebumps to a field of tiny rhinoceros horns, we get the feeling that the atmosphere has changed and that now we are in the presence of madness'.[36] Deleuze and Guattari's implication here, which is in fact a cornerstone of schizoanalysis as a whole, is that *there is a difference in kind, not degree*, between the perception of a single rhinoceros horn and a field of rhinoceros horns. As such, the latter cannot be reduced to the former – a multiplicity of horns cannot be treated as though it were effectively, much less affectively, the same as a single horn, or what amounts to the same thing as the sum of multiple horns. This is what I mean by the separation of the diachronic from the synchronic – a single horn can be construed as an analogue of the phallus or the penis, but an entire field of horns cannot; it demands that we see it as the irruption of a new system of meaning.

The focus of Deleuze and Guattari's critique of Freud's handling of the Wolf-Man case is his reading of the Wolf-Man's famous dream of five wolves in a tree outside his bedroom window from when he was very young and still living on the family estate in Russia. He later painted a picture of his dream, which today hangs in Freud's former London home (now a museum). There are two key features of the dream about which their views diverge: first, the significance of the number of wolves; and second, the significance of the fact that it is wolves and not some other creature. For Freud, the fact that there are five wolves in the tree is essentially immaterial because his interpretive methodology enables him to explain that number away and end up with the equation wolf=daddy as we always knew that he would. The actual number of wolves is just an interpretive inconvenience for Freud. By contrast, for Deleuze and Guattari, the number of wolves is *crucial* inasmuch that it indicates the presence of a pack, or rather a multiplicity, of wolves that cannot be reduced to a single figure, i.e. wolf=daddy. Freud, they say, 'obviously knows nothing about the fascination exerted by wolves and the meaning of their silent call, the call to become-wolf'.[37] This brings us to the second point of divergence, where matters are much less clear-cut. For Freud the fact that it is wolves outside the Wolf-Man's bedroom is significant only to the degree that by virtue of their threatening nature they can stand duty as representatives of his castrating father. But any other similarly imposing – i.e. castrating – animal could serve the same purpose, so the specific characteristics that comprise the wolfness of the wolves is unimportant to Freud. The wolf is simply an effective semiotic vehicle for visualizing the father in an affective manner.

For Deleuze and Guattari, though, the opposite is the case: the wolfness of the wolves is decisive inasmuch that wolves are pack animals and therefore inconceivable except as a multiplicity. However, this is where things become blurry because despite all their bluster about Freud's failure to grasp the significance of the wolves *as* wolves Deleuze and Guattari are really only interested in two aspects of the wolfness of the wolves: their pack nature and their wild status as undomesticated 'non-oedipal' animals. But even that overstates the case because they declare themselves to be uninterested in characteristics. 'The wolf is not fundamentally a characteristic or a certain number of characteristics; it is a wolfing.'[38] This does not mean that characteristics are irrelevant. Deleuze and Guattari acknowledge both that they are useful, in a scientific sense, and important in a clinical sense (the Wolf-Man's fascination for wolves would not make sense in their absence). But, in contrast to psychoanalysis, characteristics are not considered decisive, they do not serve an interpretive function. 'The elements of the pack are only imaginary "dummies", the characteristics of the pack are only symbolic entities.'[39] Deleuze and Guattari reject the idea that the wolf is simply a stand-in for the father, but they do not for all that reject the idea that the wolves might stand for something besides themselves. But it is not their specific animal characteristics that matter. As such, the animal is never encountered for itself, but always as the avatar of what might usefully be described as an inner psychological tension. The wolf, they go on to say, is 'the instantaneous apprehension of a multiplicity in a given region', as such it is 'not a representative, a substitute, but an *I feel*. I feel myself becoming a wolf, one wolf among others, on the edge of the pack.'[40] It is, in other words, a strange imperative, a feeling of transformation (and by implication a feeling of undoing) that has manifested as a wolf-feeling, at least in this instance.

It is a very peculiar form of feeling. Even as the Wolf-Man feels as though he is turning into a wolf, he also knows that he is not actually about to do so. It is *this* feeling, this strange imperative, that becoming seeks to conceptualize and name. The key to understanding becoming is to see that its utterances cannot be approached from a diachronic perspective: one cannot trace one's way back to the original source of meaning – i.e. from wolves via goats to daddy. Rather, in a synchronic manner, one must follow the transformations across the plane of immanence 'like a nomad' noting the various thresholds the subject crosses as they simultaneously lose their 'old' self and acquire a constantly changing 'new' self. Deleuze and Guattari refer to these thresholds as borders. Becoming, they say, constitutes a phenomenon of 'bordering' because it constantly propels a us towards a new metamorphosis – the wolves become wasps, then bees, and so on.[41] The wolves do not transmogrify into wasps or butterflies or penises or anuses or whatever, rather they are simply replaced as the constitutive elements of the Wolf-Man's multiplicity.[42] The change of elements in a given multiplicity is what Deleuze and Guattari mean by becoming. If the Wolf-Man is said to be fascinated by wolves, or wasps, it should not be thought that these creatures exist anywhere except inside his head. This is because the multiplicity that fascinates him (indeed all of us) is the 'multiplicity dwelling within us.'[43] What fascinates us is first of all a movement, a turbulence even, within us. This fascination for multiplicity is neither a projection nor an introjection (two psychoanalytic concepts Deleuze and

Guattari explicitly reject in *Anti-Oedipus*), but a state of being in which inside and outside no longer have any meaning.[44]

The multiplicity – wolves, wasps, whatever – is a figuration, for the want of a better word, of the libido – it is how the libido presents itself to us: we see wolves, but the wolves are simply the qualitative expression of the current turbulent state of the libido. This does not mean the wolves represent turbulence. We cannot interpret the meaning of the wolves by tracing a line back to something they represent. It is in fact the other way round: the turbulence manifests as a constantly changing multiplicity. It draws content into itself only to transform it and move on to something else. For Freud, the libido is a singular quantity of sexual energy that flows towards a defined object. It's fate, as it were, is decided by whether or not that object is available, socially appropriate, and receptive. Think of the Oedipal complex: the little boy's libido flows towards his mother, but this object is deemed inappropriate by society, so his energy is diverted elsewhere, and he resigns himself to accepting substitute objects. While it is well known that Deleuze and Guattari reject the notion that the Oedipal complex is a universal explanation of how desire functions, what is not so well known is that they also reject the restricted way Freud conceives of libido. Deleuze and Guattari vary Freud's way of conceiving libido in two crucial ways: first, they set aside the idea that libido is necessarily singular – what we might for simplicity think of as the one subject one libido theory – in favour of a multi-channel idea of libido (i.e. multiplicity) – the one subject many libidos theory; second, rather than conceive it as flowing towards an object, they conceive it as a flow (or flows) without an object as such. 'Freud himself recognizes the multiplicity of libidinal "currents" that coexist in the Wolf-Man. That makes it all the more surprising that he treats the multiplicities of the unconscious as he does.'[45] Freud wants to reduce everything to the One, the father, the mother, me, but Deleuze and Guattari want to do the opposite: they want to think how it is possible for these multiple currents to flow side by side and, more importantly, to combine with other flows to produce new currents.

Slepian and the Anxiety of Becoming

The diachronic does not simply disappear when one embarks upon a journey of becoming across the strange steppes of the plane of immanence. It haunts the plane of immanence like a spectre that threatens to arrest the flow of becoming with its powers of guilt, self-consciousness, self-reproach and so on. This is the lesson of the Slepian case, which has received comparatively little attention. The Slepian case, if it can be called that, is drawn from a short story 'Fils de chien' written by Valdimir Slepian published in *Minuit* in 1974. Like the Wolf-Man, whose real name is Sergei Pankejeff, Slepian was a Russian émigré and artist. Although born a generation later than the Wolf-Man he was just as keen to escape the Bolsheviks, albeit for different reasons. He didn't come from an aristocratic family like the Wolf-Man, but his family was nevertheless persecuted by the Soviet state. Slepian formulates his protagonist's problem as follows: 'I'm hungry, always hungry, a man should not be so hungry, so I'll have to become a dog – but how?'[46] It cannot be achieved by either imitation or analogy – it is not enough to look or act like a dog in order to become-dog. To do so is to run the risk 'of finding yourself "playing" the animal, the domestic Oedipal animal, Miller going bow-wow and taking a bone'.[47] This is the second rule of becoming: *the opposite of becoming is play*. If by 'play' we mean pretending, or even more strongly, fantasizing, then it should be clear this cannot be what becoming means because it would return us directly to psychoanalysis. Becoming is a serious business which turns to humiliation when its magic spell is broken, and the subject realizes they are 'play-acting'. Becoming is not acting, or imitating, or even performing, it has more of a kick than that, but as Derrida has shown, particularly in his work on performativity, it is impossible to forestall in an absolute way the return of the non-serious. This is, then, the inner anxiety of becoming. The feeling that one is simply play-acting, even when one is in the throes of becoming, can be interpreted, I would suggest, as the sign of the lingering influence of the plane of organization.

As we've seen, becoming is an compulsion – a strange imperative – that torments the subject, forcing them to either turn towards the body without organs and withdraw from life as Artaud did, or find the means to meet its demands and thereby convert the torment into something productive: a way of meeting life. Slepian is tormented by hunger, but the hunger seems somehow unreasonable, inhuman even, such that it is not merely a matter of finding enough to eat. The inhuman quality of the hunger seems to demand that he become-animal as the only way to 'make sense' of his feelings. Because only a dog could be this hungry! This is an eminently practical problem, which requires a practical solution in the form of an assemblage. Slepian's approach is practical but, as we'll see, doomed to fail, where failure means abandoning the attempt at the point where it would become a simple charade, lacking seriousness:

> Slepian gets the idea of using shoes to solve his problem, the artifice of the shoes. If I wear shoes on my hands, then their elements will enter into a new relation, resulting in the *affect* or becoming [note the equivalence] I seek. But how will I be able to tie the shoe on my second hand, once the first one is already occupied? With my mouth, which in turn receives an investment in the assemblage, becoming a dog muzzle, insofar as the dog muzzle is now used to tie shoes.[48]

Becoming is always double. 'For I cannot become dog without the dog becoming something else.'[49] Hands can become paws by paying the twofold price of loss of dexterity (fingers) and loss of nimbleness (dog's paws) – the artifice of the shoe can thus be understood as a kind of sobriety, as Deleuze and Guattari might put it, that attains the desired effect at the cost of a loss of affordance. The results are obviously at their most successful when it comes to the mouth, since the human's mouth and the dog's mouth are not that different in terms of what they can and can't do (we even have canine teeth with which to tear flesh). And the human mouth becomes more canine-like when our hands are denied their tactility. However, everything grinds to a halt with the tail. 'The tail would have to be invested, forced to exhibit elements common to the sexual organ and the caudal appendage [in German and French 'tail' (*Schwanz*/*queue*) is slang for penis], so that the former would be taken up in the becoming-dog assemblage of the man at the same time as the latter were taken up in a becoming of the dog, in another becoming that would also be part of the assemblage.'[50] In short, because the penis cannot *become* a tail without also ceasing to be a penis in this assemblage Slepian's plan fails and his becoming-dog is stillborn and his otherwise interesting tale descends into the mire of childhood memories. The plan isn't a complete failure, however, because it is by failing to become-dog that he is returned to his childhood memories in the way that he is. As such, one can even say failure was part of the plan from the outset.

This in turn raises a different problem, namely whether or not becoming is voluntary or involuntary. The answer to this question is unclear, which is perhaps why it is rarely – if ever – considered, because Deleuze and Guattari appear to equivocate on this issue. In the case of Slepian, which admittedly is based on a fictional short story rather than an actual case history, his becoming-dog is an experimental answer to the problem of being constantly hungry. While the feeling of constant hunger may be involuntary inasmuch as it is perfectly possible for there to be an underlying organic cause, his way of responding to it would appear to be voluntary. But perhaps looks are deceiving because one would think the obvious response to constant hunger, especially if it has or is felt to have an organic cause, would be either to eat or to seek medical treatment and perhaps resolve it with medication. The decision to instead become-dog in response to persistent hunger is then a rather curious, one might say aberrational or even pathological, course of action for Slepian to take, suggesting perhaps that his becoming-animal was involuntary after all. This is important because it influences how we think about affect and more especially the desire for certain types of effects. For it seems to me that insofar as the assemblage replaces the psychoanalytic notion of the drive it needs to be considered under the sign of compulsion (remembering that in French psychoanalysis the word for 'drive' is *pulsion*). The effects we seek are necessary to us in some way.[51] As I discussed in the previous chapter, assemblages always have a purpose: their effects are intended (in the phenomenological sense).

Slepian has a conscious goal in mind: become-dog. This is not something one finds in any of the other examples Deleuze and Guattari discuss, with the possible exception of the masochist (*Equus eroticus*) who seems to want to be treated like a horse. There are in fact two different cases of masochism discussed by Deleuze and Guattari in *A Thousand Plateaus*, but only one of which seems to follow the path of becoming-animal, hence the added designation *Equus eroticus*. The two cases are drawn from the work of neuropsychiatrist and psychoanalyst Michel de M'Uzan and the eminent French psychiatrist Roger Dupouy. Referring to a 1929 case history written up by the latter, Deleuze and Guattari quote extensively from the account the patient – identified only as 'the masochist' (*Equus eroticus*) – provides of his 'programme' (M'Uzan's word), i.e. his instructions to the equestrian-mistress (as Deleuze and Guattari designate her). 'At night, put on the bridle and attach my hands more tightly, either to the bit with the chain, or to the big belt right after returning from the bath. Put on the harness right away also, the reins and thumbscrews, and attach the thumbscrews to the harness [. . .] The master will never approach the horse without the crop, and without using it. If the animal should display impatience or rebelliousness, the reins will be drawn tighter, the master will grab them and give the beast a good thrashing.'[52]

What is going on here? It may appear that the masochist is imitating a horse, an impression compounded by their self-identification as 'horse', 'beast' and 'animal', but that is not what is going on according to Deleuze and Guattari. And just in case we are tempted to follow a Freudian script they also explicitly rule out the idea that the dominatrix can be treated as a stand-in for either the mother or father.

The masochist wants to 'tame' or even 'destroy' his own instincts and replace them with the already dominated forces of the horse. His reasoning is similar to Slepian's. He wants to be trained as a horse is trained. He wants his instincts to be dominated and subdued, or better yet regulated and channelled. The horse does as it is commanded and as a consequence its 'wild' forces are converted into 'transmitted' forces that have considerably more power – to pull a plough, carry a rider, charge into battle and so on – when viewed from the perspective of action. The real task of the dominatrix then is to bring about this conversion of forces within the space of the assemblage the masochist constructs. Becoming-horse in this context means occupying a subject position, that of a well-disciplined horse, and by doing so enable the generation of a particular set of affects – which should be designated as body-without-organs effects because they attract his desire and retroactively legitimate his process – the masochist associates with horses, e.g. being shackled by a bit, bridle and harness, but also quivering submissively before a crop. It is difficult to shake the impression that this is a form of imitation and in that regard it runs the constant risk of disintegrating into sheer play-acting. The rigorous distinction between becoming and play that Deleuze and Guattari draw is extremely useful in helping us to understand the concept because it makes at least two things clear: first, that becoming is involuntary – one does not enter a becoming on a whim; second, that even in the midst of a becoming episode (if we can call it that) the subject remains sufficiently self-aware to recognize that their actions may somehow be embarrassing. We can perhaps interpret the latter as the lingering influence of the plane of organization.

A more affirmative case of becoming-animal, one that shows the way assemblages are deployed to 'balance' the opposing trajectories of the two planes, is to be found in Deleuze and Guattari's critique of Freud's only case history of a child, Little Hans. 'Little Hans's horse is not representative but affective. It is not a member of a species but an element or individual in a machinic assemblage: draft horse-omnibus-street.'[53] The horse referred to here is the horse in Little Hans's head not the horse on the street; it is the horse as it is apprehended by Little Hans and woven into his anxiety-assemblage. 'It is defined by a list of active and passive affects [. . .]: having eyes blocked by blinders, having a bit and bridle, being proud, having a big pee-pee maker, pulling heavy loads, being whipped, falling, making a din with its legs, biting, etc. These affects circulate and are transformed within the assemblage: what a horse "can do".[54] This litany of affects is inspired by but does not refer to an actual horse – they are not the horse's affects; they are Little Hans's affects. They are derived from Little Hans's perception of horses, which were a common sight on Vienna's streets at the turn of the twentieth century. What makes this list of observations of horses on the street a list of affects is the fact that Little Hans draws power from them (i.e. he senses he can use them to diminish his passive affections and increase his active affections): in this combination they are capacitating for him, or rather he senses that they can be if he can form a relationship with them.

Little Hans's observations are thus confined to those aspects of the horse which enhance or diminish his power of acting. He notices their power, their pain, their expressiveness, but not their colour, their docility, their hauteur, nobility and so on that other writers notice. This is what Deleuze and Guattari mean by becoming-animal, which should not be confused with either fantasy or dream. Similarly, as we have already seen, it has nothing to do with imitating, playing, identifying with or feeling sympathetic towards animals. 'The question is whether Little Hans can endow his own elements with the [. . .] affects, that would make [those elements] become horse [. . .] Is there an as yet unknown assemblage that would be neither Hans's nor the horse's, but that of the becoming-horse of Hans?'[55] Ultimately, it is not a question of what an actual horse can do, but rather of what Little Hans can do. When the horse bares its teeth, perhaps to whinny in the street, that becomes an affect for Little Hans because he sees its expressive possibilities and wonders what he might do to similarly empower himself. 'Hans might show something else, his feet, his legs, his peepee-maker [and so on].'[56] The question this poses is whether or not it would help Little Hans, 'would it open a way out that had been previously blocked?'[57] In other words, the affects he perceives are his means of overcoming his feeling of passivity, which materializes in his case as anxiety, if he can find the means. What is crucial to note here is that, in Deleuze and Guattari's analysis of Little Hans, affects are conceived as charged segments that form multiple combinations, some of which enhance his capacity to act and others that don't. These affects are the product of his perception and as such, although they seem to relate to a horse's body, actually relate to his desiring-process, which is why Deleuze and Guattari refer to it as a form of becoming-animal.

Three Theories of Affect

The Little Hans case is additionally interesting here for the way it brings to the fore one of the more problematic aspects of Deleuze and Guattari's theory of affect that I've held off discussing in detail until now, though I did allude to it in the Introduction, namely the many inconsistencies in their actual usage of the term 'affect'. These inconsistencies, as I argued at the outset, are such that there is no logical way to resolve things in a coherent manner so that the differences between the various iterations of the term seem to be all cut from the same cloth. This is why I have approached affect in Deleuze and Guattari's work from the perspective of a unified field theory. I want to dwell on these differences for a moment now because, as I argued in the Introduction (following Jameson), they retain a sectoral validity that is useful and not something we want necessarily to wish away. Not least because in pretending that these differences don't exist and don't somehow inform Deleuze and Guattari's work is to effectively blind ourselves to their possibilities. The necessity of the unified field theory approach can be demonstrated quite easily. There are at least three different conceptions of affect in Deleuze and Guattari's work: (1) dissociated capacities; (2) mobile fragments of libido; and (3) psychological projectiles.

The first meaning of affect, which is the version affect theory recognizes, that I will label 'dissociated capacities', is itself split into two – one iteration drawn from Spinoza and the other iteration drawn from ethology, specifically Jacob Uexküll. Deleuze and Guattari treat them as synonymous, but this is poetic licence at best. 'An affect of our body is only a corporeal image, and the idea of the affection as it is in our mind an inadequate idea, an imagining. And we have yet another sort of affection. From a given idea of an affection there necessarily flow "affects" or feelings (*affectus*). Such feelings are themselves affections, or rather a new kind of affection.'[58] It is our ideas that function as affections. They indicate to us both the state of our body and any changes our body might have undergone, but they remain firmly artefacts of the mind not the muscles. These affections are passive in Spinoza's terms because the idea we form of our body in most circumstances is not explained by our power of understanding. For example, the feeling of hunger is something we 'suffer' rather than cause, as such it is not the product of our understanding, but merely a passive affection. In Spinoza's terms it is an inadequate idea. The sensations in our stomach interpreted by us as the feeling of hunger *are not affects*, they only become affects once we form an image of them in our mind and develop ideas in response to that image. Here we might think of the infant who experiences a certain discomfort in their stomach and cries but does not know – we assume – what causes that discomfort but ceases to cry when they are offered food. In time they will close the loop and realize that the discomfort they're experiencing means they require food, but in their earliest days it is experienced as discomfort without cause.

It is easy to see why Spinoza regarded childhood an 'abject state': it is characterized by passive affections.[59] Affect in Uexküll, at least as Deleuze and Guattari characterize it, is – if anything – an even more abject state than childhood is according to Spinoza because it is not merely passive, it is instinctual, literally unthinking. The famous example of the tick, which Deleuze and Guattari refer to on a number of occasions, reduces affect to an innate capacity, which is certainly not how Spinoza treats affect. 'For example, the Tick, attracted by light, hoists itself up to the tip of the branch; it is sensitive to the smell of mammals, and it lets itself fall when one passes beneath the branch; it digs into its skin, at the least hairy place it can find. Just three affects; the rest of the time the tick sleeps.'[60] The fact they think ticks live in trees tends to suggest Deleuze and Guattari didn't read Uexküll all that attentively, although it doesn't thereby vitiate what they propose. The apparent automatism of the tick's response is perhaps of interest to Deleuze and Guattari as a model for a certain type of becoming that happens under the sign of the strange imperative which compels action in an unthinking, unconscious, way. As is the case in becoming, the tick's actions are precipitated by an external trigger. It is nevertheless clearly not the same conception of affect that one finds in their account of Spinoza, despite the fact that they seem to regard Uexküll to be Spinozist in some way. There is no sense in Uexküll that the tick's capacities are an affection in the mind. What they draw from Uexküll though, which is consistent with Spinoza to a certain degree, is a way of reimagining the body as a set of 'dissociated capacities' rather than body parts that can be combined as elements of an assemblage. This in turn enables a re-engineering of the Lacanian concept of the drive, shifting the focus from specific body parts to capacities that, among other things, has a de-oedipalizing effect on how we think about the body.[61]

This version of affect is clearly not the same as the version found in their account of how the body without organs works I will label 'mobile fragments of libido'. Here affects are classified as becomings.[62] Returning to the example of the masochist, they say that his goal with the training-assemblage is to create a body without organs on which only intensities (i.e. mobile fragments of libido) can circulate.[63] I have already discussed this example at length, so I won't belabour the point. I will simply note that in this example intensities are described as affects, and in turn they're linked to becomings, which they characterize in terms of a change in the subject's microperceptions. 'No longer are there acts to explain, dreams or phantasies to interpret, childhood memories to recall, words to make signify; instead, there are colours and sounds, becomings and intensities.'[64] This is no longer a matter of capacities, it has solely to do with the movement of libido. It is true that there are aspects of their account of masochism that turn on the notion of 'dissociated capacities' I have just outlined, but they do not use affect in that sense in their discussion of the way the masochism-assemblage works. For instance, one of the effects the masochist seeks by means of his elaborate training-assemblage is the transformation of the woman as mistress into a series of eroticized capacities: boots rather than legs, fear rather than boots, and so on.[65]

The third version of affect is in many ways the most confounding because it directly – or at least appears to – contradict the idea that becoming, as an 'I feel', can be considered an affect. Here we need to look at the passage in the war-machine chapter where they propose to make a qualitative – not quantitative – distinction between weapons and tools. This case study is additionally interesting because it also makes it clear that Deleuze and Guattari do not consider the physical properties of things to be in any way decisive in determining the nature of an assemblage. The properties of material things only interest them insofar as they are apprehended and applied by different social machines. But it is the *differences* between the social machines that is of primary importance to them, not the differences in the properties of the material objects themselves. They set aside material differences right from the outset as not being sufficient in themselves to draw a sharp delineation between weapons and tools. And it is worth adding here that Deleuze and Guattari frequently insist that assemblages have 'cutting-edges', which is to say they are not amorphous or open-ended, but always rigorously distinct in their formation.

Of course, an extrinsic differentiation between weapons and tools can always be made on the basis of usage but Deleuze and Guattari suggest this is a relatively weak form of distinction because it does not 'preclude a general convertibility between the two groups'.[66] It may even be the case, they admit, that an intrinsic distinction between weapons and tools is out of reach because it appears that they share the same (machinic) phylum. They nevertheless insist there are internal differences between the weapons-assemblage and the tools-assemblage that, even if they do not rise to the level of intrinsic differences, are still worth considering because of the light it sheds on the nature of the war machine as they want to define it. In other words, they are saying that even if two objects – one classified as a tool and another classified as a weapon – are identical in a *quantitative* sense (i.e. a material sense), they can and should still be regarded as different in a *qualitative* sense (i.e. an affective sense). Here one might compare the warrior's battle-axe with the forester's tree-felling axe: materially they are very similar, but in design and purpose they are very different, right down to the filigree that decorates the weapon but is absent in the tool. The differential method, as Deleuze and Guattari call it, uses qualitative differences to draw distinctions between different types of assemblages, in this case the weapon-assemblage and the tool-assemblage.

'As a first approximation,' they write, 'weapons have a privileged relation with projection. Anything that throws or is thrown is fundamentally a weapon, and propulsion is its *essential* movement. The weapon is ballistic; the very notion of the "problem" is related to the war machine. The more mechanisms of projection a tool has, the more it behaves like a weapon, potentially or simply metaphorically.'[67] To which they add the important qualification that even though tools can also be shown to have mechanisms of projection, they constantly seek to compensate for this, or else adapt them to other ends, so that on balance they are predominantly introceptive. The weapon also has an essential relation with speed. 'It is yet another essential contribution of Paul Virilio to have stressed this weapon–speed complementarity: the weapon invents speed, or the discovery of speed invents the weapon (the projective character of weapons is the result).'[68] This in turn opens still another line of differentiation, this time between hunting and warfare. 'As Virilio says, war in no way appears when man applies to man the relation of the hunter to the animal, but on the contrary when he captures the force of the hunted animal and enters an entirely new relation to man, that of war (enemy, no longer prey).'[69]

War is a very different kind of violence to hunting – it is not 'blow by blow' or 'once and for all', it is enduring, unlimited; it is the violence of raising animals for the sole purpose of their exploitation. This is the bloodthirsty reality of the becoming-animal of the war machine. 'It is therefore not surprising,' they say, 'that the war machine was the invention of the animal-raising nomads.'[70] Once captured, speed becomes a 'free or independent variable' that disrupts the equilibrium of any situation from which it is abstracted. This does not mean that it cannot give rise to situations in which its disruptive force becomes the cause of immobility, as happened in the First World War when machine guns and artillery forced the stalemate of trench warfare that was only broken when movement was rediscovered with the tank.[71] It could still be argued, though, that this kind of speed is comparable to the speed one finds in the use of tools we generally refer to as work – for instance, the hydraulic nail gun has all but rendered the hammer obsolete – but Deleuze and Guattari counter this objection by noting that 'there is too much of a tendency to think in terms of *quantities* of movement, instead of seeking *qualitative* models'.[72]

In contrast to the weapon, the tool is introceptive: 'it prepares a matter from a distance, in order to bring it to a state of equilibrium or to appropriate it for a form of *interiority*'.[73] Again, it is worth adding here that this is precisely the opposite of DeLanda's claim that assemblages do not concern relations of interiority. Consider the example of the construction of a house. The frame of the house draws materials together and creates not just an interior space, but also an interiorizing relation between all the materials. This point can perhaps be seen more clearly by considering the abstract idea of a house.[74] What must a house contain? Must it have an indoor toilet, kitchen, bedroom and so on in order to be a house? Is it still a house if it lacks any of these things? What are the limits? Can it have a kitchen but no bedroom? A bedroom and no kitchen? The point I want to make here is that all of these relations are necessarily relations of interiority. It is true that the materials can be separated from any particular construction and used elsewhere but that does not mean that when they are fastened together that the relations between them are exclusively exterior as DeLanda claims because there is nothing stopping them from also being bound in a relation of interiority. The irony here, if that's the right word, is that DeLanda fails to draw the obvious conclusion from the point he insists on: if relations are external to their terms, then it cannot be the interaction of the properties of the terms that defines the nature of the assemblage.

'One could also say that the tool encounters resistances, to be conquered or put to use, while the weapon has to do with counterattack, to be avoided or invented (the counterattack is in fact the precipitating and inventive factor in the war machine, to the extent that it is not simply reducible to a quantitative rivalry or defensive parade).'[75] As they go onto clarify, 'counterattack implies a rush or change of speed that breaks the equilibrium', which is not the same as overcoming resistance because it implies the disruption of a given situation rather than its cashing out.[76] To put it another way, the tool generates surplus value, which is cashed out in the moment, but the weapon does not. 'Work is a motor cause that meets resistances, operates upon the exterior, is consumed and spent in its effect, and must be renewed from one moment to the next. Free action is also a motor cause, but one that has no resistance to overcome, operates only upon the mobile body itself, is not consumed in its effect, and continues from one moment to the next.'[77] Work necessarily has a point of application, a punctum where force exerted, whereas 'free action' applies to a smooth, non-punctuated space. The weapon is vortical whereas the tool is linear. 'It is as though the weapon were moving, self-propelling, while the tool is moved.'[78] Tools do not define work, any more than weapons define war, they presuppose work just as weapons presuppose war (or at least its constant threat). Both tool and weapon remain undetermined unless they are related to the assemblage that presupposes them.[79]

Deleuze and Guattari go on to separate the tool-assemblage (work) and the weapon-assemblage (war machine) in terms of a highly differentiated notion of desire:

> The work regime is inseparable from an organization and development of Form, corresponding to which is the formation of the subject. This is the passional regime of feeling as 'the form of the worker'. Feeling implies an evaluation of matter and its resistances, a direction (*sens*, also 'meaning') to form its developments, an economy of force and its displacements, an entire gravity.[80]

This is to be contrasted with the war machine:

> [T]he regime of the war machine is on the contrary that of affects, which relate only to the moving body in itself, to speeds and compositions of speeds among elements. Affect is the active discharge

of emotion, the counterattack, whereas feeling is an always displaced, retarded, resisting emotion. Affects are projectiles just like weapons; feelings are introceptive like tools.[81]

These two passages are among the most extraordinary in the whole of Deleuze and Guattari's work. The model of affect presented here is not developed elsewhere in their work, but it is nevertheless highly suggestive because it seems to indicate that the concept of the war-machine should in fact be interpreted in a psychological light. To put it another way, it points towards a dimension of the psychical agency of affect, as I have called it, which is not often considered, namely its capacity for aggressivity. This iteration of affect only makes sense if we subsume it under the umbrella of a psychical agency, otherwise it contradicts the idea that becoming as an 'I feel' relates to affect. While these three versions of affect discussed here are not necessarily antithetical, neither can they be treated as synonymous. Nor do they cancel each other out such that one could determine that one version was ultimately superior to the others. I tend to think Deleuze and Guattari would reject both of those approaches, which leaves us with Jameson's model of the dialectic as the only viable means of going forward without having to make one of these 'poor' choices. It is, therefore, the only way we can speak of Deleuze and Guattari's notion of affect and not find ourselves at cross-purposes at almost every turn because the version of affect that affect theory has embraced is but one of three possible versions in their work. The differences between them matter and properly framed are useful to retain.

5 MODELLING AFFECT

The death of a social machine has never been heralded by a disharmony or a dysfunction; on the contrary, social machines make a habit of feeding on the contradictions they give rise to, on the crises they provoke, on the anxieties they engender, and on the infernal operations they regenerate.[1]

If contemporary politics can only be understood in terms of affect, as Brian Massumi has long insisted (a position I agree with even if I don't necessarily agree with his account of how to go about it), that is because it is affect that feeds on the contradictions of society. It can do this because affect, unlike reason, does not experience contradictions as disabling, indeed it doesn't really experience them as contradictions. As such, the key to understanding contemporary politics is the problem of what I have called the composition of affect. There is no better example of the need for a model of political analysis sensitive to the workings of affect than the election campaigns and presidencies of Donald Trump, which have been marked by so many contradictions it is hard to know how to untangle them much less where to begin. This should not be mistaken for uncritical partisanship for the 'other' side I hasten to add. The Democrat challenger Kamala Harris offered nothing but more of the same bitter neoliberal gruel Biden had served up for the previous four years, itself the warmed-over seconds from the Obama years. She did not even propose to intervene to end the atrocity of Israel's attack on Gaza, a fact that perhaps cost her the election because she lost the Muslim vote in crucial districts. Little wonder then that the dominant voter category in the 2024 US election was the non-voter. As Sartre put it in 1945 in the novel *The Reprieve*, 'It must be rather grim to hope for nothing except that life might continue in its present course.'[2] Trump, at least, promised something more exhilarating than that! The fact that anyone found his rhetoric credible, let alone inspiring, is a problematic that deserves careful consideration because in all likelihood it is a harbinger of things to come. We seem to have blundered into an age of politics bereft of truth, ideas and any semblance of the now forgotten utopian ideal that government should serve the interests of its people.

The Trump Assemblage?

Like many people I found it difficult to fathom why anyone would vote for a reality TV hack and grifter like Trump the first time in 2016 and simply baffling that they would vote for him a second, and indeed a third time, after the appalling way he handled the Covid-19 epidemic, letting hundreds of thousands of people die entirely preventable deaths.[3] I have read a great many accounts of how and why Trump was elected, all of them persuasive in their different ways, without ever being fully satisfying. In part I think this is because they tend to lack a theory of complexity capable of registering the conflicting values at least some Trump voters must have in deciding to vote for him. Despite a reputation for misogyny – multiple wives, mistresses, allegations of sexual impropriety, outright admissions of sexual impropriety (the infamous 'grab them by the pussy' comment), hush money paid to prostitutes and so on – Trump still managed to win the support of substantial numbers of women voters and Christian voters, which tends to suggest that people's political leanings are not decided by single issues, or what are sometimes called 'rational choices', but stem rather from something much more inchoate. Similarly, Trump received support from construction workers despite his long and well-documented history of stiffing his employees, a scenario for which the word 'contradiction' does not seem adequate. Trump even had the gall to present himself as the construction workers' friend.[4] Probably the most convincing, and certainly the most insightful in terms of the economic determinants of Trump's popularity, is Melinda Cooper's magisterial *Counterrevolution*, but this still tends to shape its account around interests rather than desires and does not give an explanation of how the many contradictions of Trump's public persona were 'worked through' on a psychosocial level by his supporters.[5]

The assumption made by many that only the poor, the stupid and the uneducated voted for Trump is neither true nor helpful. It may be that people were misguided in believing Trump would deliver on his promises, but that isn't a matter of stupidity or ignorance so much as it is a matter of desire. Desire, as Deleuze and Guattari argue, operates on multiple levels, such that we're capable of desiring antithetical things without any sense of conflict. I will explore this idea in more detail below when we turn to the theoretical matter at hand, namely the composition of affect. For now, I will say it is my view that for the most part people were not deceived by Trump, they wanted what he purported to be selling and, just as importantly, they assumed they were somehow immune to the pain he promised to rain upon others. Viewed from the perspective of affect rather than policy proposals, Trump offered his supporters an image of America in which individualism reigns supreme such that opinion and feeling, however half-baked and ill-thought, trumps science and reason. If you don't believe in vaccines that is your right and no elitist scientist or health professional can claim to know better, or so this thinking goes. In this regard, Deleuze and Guattari's endorsement of Reich's account of Nazi Germany applies fully to Trump's supporters today: 'no, the masses were not innocent dupes; at a certain point, under a certain set of conditions, they *wanted* fascism, and it is this perversion of the desire of the masses that needs to be accounted for'.[6] The question isn't whether Trump represents a return of fascism – clearly in some sense it does, as I will discuss below – but rather what kind of a transformation (i.e. perversion) of desire does his politics entail?[7]

To my mind, this is a problem of the composition of affect because what is at stake is the problem of how people can accommodate the many contradictions in his political rhetoric, some aspects of which they may neither agree with nor like. Many people writing about Trump's apparently anomalous supporter base (Christians, women, blue-collar workers, the educated middle class, people of colour, and so on) have found inspiration in Deleuze and Guattari's appropriation of Spinoza which prefaces the comment quoted above about the desire for fascism: 'the fundamental problem of political philosophy is still precisely the one that Spinoza saw so clearly, and that Wilhelm Reich discovered: "Why do men fight for their servitude as stubbornly as though it were salvation?"'[8] Ultimately, Deleuze and Guattari do not answer this question, but they do propose an answer to the perhaps more concretely philosophical problem of how it is possible that people's desire can be turned against them. Their answer to this latter question takes us to the problem of the composition of affect.

They do not use the word 'affect' in this context, but it is nevertheless clear that it is this psychical agency that they turn to in order to explain the many paradoxes of political desire. They reject the idea that this problem can be adequately dealt with via the concept of ideology, which they define in very narrow terms as a process of deception and false consciousness (these states of being are essentially opposite sides of the same coin).

Against Ideology

I tend to think that Deleuze and Guattari's abhorrence of the concept of ideology is misguided in this regard because in many ways what they do in their own work is offer a richer version of it. I see their rejection of ideology as a particularly telling instance of the type of conceptual translation I described in the Introduction whereby a standard critical term is replaced by a range of others – plane of immanence, plane of organization, the assemblage – that cover the same territory, but do so in a new way. While this renders the 'old' term obsolete as far as they are concerned, they obviously feel its return has to be constantly warded off with apotropaic statements. In essence, then, they offer a different answer to the same question ideology answers, which is: Why do people act against their own interests? This becomes clear when one looks at their specific objection to the concept of ideology and their proposed workaround. Deleuze and Guattari are unequivocal in expressing their distaste for the concept of ideology. It is 'execrable' they say on more than one occasion because 'it hides the real problems'.[9] The 'real problem' that the concept of ideology hides, in their view, which is the principal reason they reject what we might call the vulgar Marxist conception of ideology as a process of deception and false consciousness, is that it depends on what they hold to be a spurious separation between the infrastructure (economic base) and the superstructure (the social and cultural milieu). It has to be emphasized here that the version of ideology they reject is very much an artefact of its time and its place, i.e. Paris in the 1960s and 70s, for which the name Althusser can stand as the general exemplar of what they had in mind.

That there were many other ways of conceiving ideology available elsewhere in the world at that time seems to have escaped their notice.[10] For this reason we need to be careful not to 'universalize' their objections to ideology and buy into the mistaken view that ideology in general is a bad concept. We can trace the logic of their critique of ideology for its own sake, but only as a step along the way to a better understanding of how and why they felt the need to re-engineer it in the manner that they do, rather than as a prelude to throwing out the concept altogether. The model of ideology they reject holds that desire does not invest directly in the economic base, which is deemed to be too abstract and too mechanical to attract desire in and of itself. Instead, desire is invested in the superstructure, namely culture in the broadest sense of the word, which is variously conceived as a symptom or expression of the base, or more usually as a lure that captures desire and prevents us from ever seeing the truth of our economic situation. This is sometimes framed as alienation, whereby we seem to have lost the capacity to even understand the economic base sufficiently to invest in it directly. The less charitable form of this is the notion of 'false consciousness' which holds that even when we think we understand the economic underpinnings of our daily lives we are in fact deluding ourselves that we really know what is going on.[11]

Trump's obsession with tariffs would seem to both confirm and refute this view of ideology. On the one hand, it seems fairly clear that most Trump voters did not understand the economic effects tariffs would have; in many cases, it seems that some did not even grasp that it would make a great many products more expensive. Those who thought that the tariffs would boost the American economy and therefore serve their interests were clearly prey to a form of false consciousness because although they had convinced themselves they understood the economic base they actually did not understand it all. By the same token, however, the way desire is invested in tariffs themselves as an 'object' of desire disproves the idea that desire cannot invest directly in the base. Indeed, Trump's success would seem to hinge on having rendered the economic base desirable for itself: people *want* tariffs without fully knowing what in a practical sense it is that they desire. This might seem to confirm that this is an instance of false consciousness, but there is an important split here between the operations of desire and the operations of interest. People seem to desire tariffs in and of themselves, i.e. independently of whether or not they will further their own interests. This split between desire and interest is the cornerstone of Deleuze and Guattari's re-engineering of ideology. Their position can be summarized as follows: interest can be deceived, but desire cannot.

Deleuze and Guattari's re-engineering of ideology has three steps, two of which I have already mentioned: first, they reject the idea that desire cannot invest directly in the base; second, they draw a distinction between desire and interest and argue that only interest can be deceived; third, and perhaps most importantly, they draw a distinction between preconscious and unconscious investments. They mobilize this latter distinction in a manner I am tempted to describe as dialectical (in Jameson's sense) because they use it to theorize the coincidence of opposites which do not cancel one another out. As Guattari put it in an interview following the publication of *Anti-Oedipus*, 'We distinguish between two ways the social field's invested: preconsciously invested by interests and unconsciously invested by desire. The way interests are invested can be truly revolutionary, while at the same time leaving in place unconscious investments of desire that aren't revolutionary, that may even be fascistic.'[12] That is to say, viewed from the perspective of desire people's political allegiances can be – and often are – completely contradictory (as Deleuze and Guattari acknowledge). But 'they' do not experience it as contradictory, or even as conflicted, because of the multilayered way desire invests the social field.

Neoliberalism as it has evolved over the last forty years has been particularly effective at capitalizing – quite literally – on this split between desire and interest. Perhaps the most egregious instance of this has been the transformation of the family home into an asset by means of tax incentives combined with easy and cheap credit. This has led to skyrocketing house prices in some cities – Auckland, London, New York, Sydney and Vancouver are among the worst effected – thus creating an unbridgeable generational divide between those who bought their houses before the boom and those who will never be able to buy a house because of the boom. Housing booms appear to serve the interests of homeowners by creating a substantial asset, but in reality they are a burden – the large loans required to buy into the market soak up disposable income and anchor people politically and geographically to their mortgages. Interest rates take on a political significance out of all proportion with other political concerns. And to ensure that no government gives into political pressure and goes soft on interest rates central banks have been created that answer to no higher power than 'the market'.[13]

Booms are a matter of desire not interest. This has long been recognized by neoliberal economists. In 1978, the future chair of the US Federal Reserve Alan Greenspan described the impact of rising house prices as a 'wealth effect' (which I would designate as a body without organs effect) whereby people felt richer despite a static or even declining income:[14]

> The task of schizoanalysis is therefore to reach the investments of unconscious desire of the social field, insofar as they are differentiated from the preconscious investments of desire, and insofar as they are not merely capable of counteracting them, but also of *coexisting with them in opposite modes*.[15]

Affect operates on multiple levels at once. I use the word 'level' here for the want of a better word, but it is in many ways inadequate. This doubtless explains why Deleuze and Guattari never seemed to have felt the need to restrict themselves to using just one conceptual language to articulate the operations of affect. Indeed, as we've seen, they make use of several, which adds to the complexity of reading their work, but also underscores the importance of recognizing the way they mobilize an idea of translation to constantly rewrite and rework existing conceptual languages, including their own. As I have already argued, Deleuze and Guattari divide affect into two separate planes – plane of immanence or consistency and plane of organization – joined by an indefinite number of assemblages that serve as relays between them. These planes are themselves further divided into distinct operational sectors (again for want of a better word). The plane of immanence, as we've seen, is composed of a multiplicity of bodies without organs, while the plane of organization is composed of a multiplicity of abstract machines. Thus far I have tended to focus on the role the plane of immanence plays in structuring affect, now I want to turn to the plane of organization, and more specifically the abstract machine. It would be fair to say, I think, that the abstract machine has received comparatively little attention in the critical literature on Deleuze and Guattari. This neglect is impossible to justify because neither the assemblage nor the body without organs make sense in its absence. This is particularly apparent when, as is the case here, we're interested in trying to understand in an historical way how the structure of the present moment came about.

The People Are Missing

The abstract machine can be dramatized, which is to say made vivid and alive, by pairing it with another concept from Deleuze and Guattari's arsenal that should be regarded as its binary opposite, the notion that the 'people are missing'. My suggestion is, which may be phrased in Freudian fashion as follows, there where the people were missing the abstract machine will be. The abstract machine, as we'll see, always precedes the assemblage, but it can only be actualized by assemblages when the people are there. 'This is not a proposition one proves,' as Jameson once put it, 'rather, one seeks [. . .] to demonstrate the interest of presupposing it, and in particular the variety of new consequences that flow from' it.[16] The 'people are missing' refers to a situation in which, for a given population (conceived in terms of nation, ethnicity, gender, political conviction, etc.), the political consciousness required to bring about social change, whether by revolution or reform, has become too fragmented and factionalized to be effective. In this situation, the artist appears to have only two choices, either to remain silent, or to cross over to the side of the powerful and speak in their voice, but according to Deleuze and Guattari Kafka identified a third possibility, which they characterize in terms of the 'minor', in which the artist produces 'the seeds of the people to come'.[17] This work neither speaks for the disempowered nor against the powerful but rather seeks to 'express potential forces' that may at some point in the future serve as a catalyst to change.[18]

When the people are missing, the artist – but also the intellectual – has no option but to try to compose a new abstract machine. There is no better illustration of this point than the situation today regarding climate change. It is clear that the artists and activists calling for action on climate change are essentially speaking to a people who are missing. The people who will act on the warnings they issue even if it means giving up 'nice things' do not yet exist. To be sure, there are small groups of isolated people who try to live off the grid, who drive electric cars, sort their recycling, and go to rallies against coal mines, but they are too few in number to bring about systematic change. More importantly, their actions are – at best – regarded by most as noble but eccentric and not as an emerging hegemonic position, which is what is actually required for large-scale change to occur. Not only that, there is a significant amount of 'sunk' carbon in off-the-grid living – fossil fuels are used in the manufacture and the distribution of most if not all the objects one needs for such a lifestyle (rainwater tanks, solar panels, batteries and so on). Even though the people are missing, the abstract machine we will need in order to change things is slowly coming into view, as are the conditions that will precipitate its actualization. It is, however, in the nature of the abstract machine that we can never fully know beforehand what will bring it into fruition. We may sense that change is coming, we may even know what change is required – e.g. the drastic reduction in CO_2 emissions – but we cannot know in advance what will render this way of thinking and seeing legitimate (body without organs) and possible (abstract machine). This is cold comfort for those of us concerned that collectively we are destroying the earth, not only for ourselves, but for every living creature, but it is better than defeat. That, at least, seems to be the gambit of Kafka's notion of the minor literature, which underpins the idea of the 'people are missing' in Deleuze's work on cinema. The abstract machine can be conceived in the absence of the people, but not actualized, which is the beauty and the tragedy of minor literature as well as minor politics.

I want to suggest, though, that Deleuze and Guattari's concept of the minor, which is utopian in every sense of the word, is insufficiently developed by Deleuze and Guattari because it does not allow for – acknowledge might be a better word – the possibility of a fascist variant. The fact that the minor mode is utopian does not preclude it from having a fascist mode, I hasten to add, because fascism is itself a utopian project inasmuch as ignites a collective energy directed towards the goal of creating a new world.[19] This isn't a reason to dismiss the notion of utopia *tout court* – Deleuze and Guattari definitely do not do that – but it does suggest that we need to treat it in a differential manner, as we do bodies without organs, separating the healthy from the unhealthy, the progressive from the murderous. It is strange that Deleuze and Guattari do not allow for a fascist form of the minor because their account of fascism as a molecular phenomenon would seem to suggest that very possibility. The minor is always a molecular form that develops in dialogue with a major form it can neither escape nor accept – Kafka could not *not* write in German, yet neither could he write in German in a German way, or as a German. He was fluent in Czech, but this wasn't *his* language, it was a bureaucratic language for him. Literally so, it was the language he used in his job as an insurance adjuster. So he had to find a way of inflecting German to create room for his own voice as a minority within a minority, namely that of a Czech German Jew. For Kafka German was a major language in a geopolitical sense, but something of a minor language in Prague where Czech was the principal language. As such, it felt like both an oppressive language – the language of a distant centre of power (for most of Kafka's life Prague was part of the Austro-Hungarian empire) – and an orphan language isolated from the main groups of German speakers. This feeling was amplified for Jews like Kafka who were 'simultaneously a part of this minority and excluded from it'.[20]

The other crucial aspect of the concept of minor politics, which Deleuze and Guattari do not dwell on, though it is plain to see, is that it consists of a unity of opposites – Kafka could not *not* write in German and he could not *not* write. This is important because it helps us to understand what I'm calling the fascist variant, which is similarly composed of a unity of opposites, or what Deleuze and Guattari prefer to call a multiplicity. The model that enables the antithetical elements to hang together is that of the substantive multiplicity. In *Anti-Oedipus* they attribute this idea to Maurice Blanchot who uses it solve the problem of how to think about the relationship between fragments, by which he means parts of a literary text, 'whose sole relationship is sheer difference – fragments that are related to one another only in that each of them is different – without having recourse either to any sort of original totality (not even one that has been lost), or to a subsequent totality that may not yet come about'.[21] Multiplicity is explicitly posed against the idea of the dialectic, which they describe as a colourless evolution 'aimed at forming a harmonious whole out of heterogeneous bits by rounding off their edges'.[22] However, this image of the dialectic is something of a caricature so we do not need to take it too seriously.

The Unity of Opposites

Schizoanalysis can be understood, then, as the attempt to try to map the various ways and means we have of both sustaining these unities and altering the structure and (most importantly) the composition of these unities. I will further observe, purely for heuristic purposes I hasten to add, that what Deleuze and Guattari have in mind with respect to the concept of multiplicity corresponds almost exactly with Jameson's notion of the dialectic which he characterizes as the unity of opposites. Jameson often illustrates this with a quote from Brecht about the ambivalent nature of Hollywood. As Brecht puts it, God economized with Hollywood and put heaven and hell in the same place. For the prosperous Hollywood is heaven, but for that very reason it is hell for the poor.[23] The experience of one does not cancel out the experience of the other and there is no possible synthesis here except in the form of a multiplicity. The edges cannot be rounded off if we want to understand Hollywood as it actually is for the people who live there. The rich constantly seek to isolate themselves from the poor, but in doing so define heaven as that which escapes hell, rather than as something particular to itself. But their escape is to comfortable prisons with high walls, razor wire, security guards and constant video surveillance. Similarly, poverty is defined as a kind of purgatory in which one lives in the shadows of these high walls and waits indefinitely and without hope for entrance into these heavenly prisons. In order to account fully for Hollywood, then, we have to see it as simultaneously heaven *and* hell.

We find another illustration of this point in F. Scott Fitzgerald's short memoir 'The Crack-up' which Deleuze and Guattari often refer to. Fitzgerald says that 'the test of a first-rate intelligence is the ability to hold two opposed ideas in the mind at the same time, and still retain the ability to function. One should, for example, be able to see things are hopeless and yet be determined to make them otherwise'.[24] This is precisely a unity of opposites – there is no sense that one feeling will cancel out the other. Indeed the beauty of it is precisely the balance between possibility and impossibility that one navigates like a high-wire artiste. A similar sentiment, affirming what must be considered as the non-paradoxical and non-contradictory coincidence of opposites that is a 'normal' state of being for many people, is found expressed in Beckett's line from the novel *The Unnamable* which Foucault recites so affectingly in the opening of his inaugural lecture at the College de France: 'I can't go on, I'll go on'.[25] In both examples antithetical sentiments sit side by side without cancelling one another out. The fact of being able to go on in no way discounts the feeling of the impossibility of going on that has to be surmounted in order to go on. Going on does not in any way repudiate the impossibility of going on either. In fact, whatever sense of personal satisfaction one derives from being able to go on is directly proportional to the strength of the feeling that it was in fact impossible to go on. Both the possibility of going on and the impossibility of going on exist side by side in a state that phenomenology calls the 'always already' (as we discussed in Chapter 1). Our feeling of hope in the face of a sense of hopelessness functions in a similar way. This is what I mean by the composition of affect – the simultaneity of potentially opposite ways of feeling that coexist in a way we experience as 'normal' rather than as 'conflicted'.

This is why Deleuze and Guattari say no society died of its contradictions. 'Capitalism has learned this, and has ceased doubting itself, while even socialists have abandoned belief in the possibility of capitalism's natural death by attrition.'[26] This is generally taken to be a critique of Hegelian forms of Marxism, which it obviously is, but one might also see it as an insight into the problem we face today, which is precisely that societies do not die of contradictions. If they did Trump would not have been possible and the revolution all Marxists have said would happen if society did not resolve its contradictions would have taken place. Deleuze and Guattari's turn to what they call schizoanalysis follows this insight: if societies do not die from contradictions, but rather seem to thrive on them, then Marxism has been looking at them the wrong way. Contradictions are not fault lines in the social machine, they are its engines, and they work precisely by breaking society down. 'And the more it breaks down, the more it schizophrenizes, the better it works, the American way.'[27] Trump supporters see no contradiction in supporting an exploitative billionaire as their champion because they think he's a dealmaker not a politician, and that politicians are corrupt and business is the only kind of truth there is in America today. That they see no contradiction in that position is precisely the problem that should concern us: it is perhaps the absence of contradictions that will cause capitalism to die of attrition because it no longer sees them as warning signs.

The fascist variant of minor politics follows a different path from the one advocated by Kafka and Deleuze and Guattari. It is not content to sow the seeds of a people yet to come, it has greater urgency than that. Fascism does not see the need to wait because it takes the view its people are not missing, they're already here, they just need to be mobilized. It knows they're not missing because fascism is always couched in terms of the resurrection of a past glory, one it says lives on 'in' us – i.e. those of 'us' already present – if only we have the courage and commitment to be 'true' to our inner 'selves'. For the Nazis it was the fantasy of the 'master race' of the proto-European people the Aryans, while for the Italian fascists it was the memory of the Roman empire that spurred them on. Trump's rallying cry 'make America great again' is similarly structured around a supposedly lost moment of glory, it just isn't clear when that moment was. It could be the so-called Gilded Age around the end of the nineteenth century when the 'self-made' billionaire oligarchs like J. P. Morgan, Andrew Carnegie, John D. Rockefeller and all the other 'Robber Barons' rose to prominence. This was also a time of reconstruction following the Civil War, immiseration and dispossession of indigenous peoples, and impoverishment for working people in the industrial cities of the north.

So it's not clear why anyone would consider it something they would want to return to, unless they were a billionaire like Trump. The other candidate is the post-Second World War boom years, which until the 1970s at least were a time of high employment and upward social mobility, especially for white Americans. Ironically it was also a peak period of unionization, something Trump's supporters claim they're opposed to. In any case, it does not need to be a real moment in time they want to return to, they simply want that sense of greatness they feel they once had and has since been lost. This is clearly an intoxicating idea to a great many voters, even if (or perhaps because) the practicalities of it are never made clear.

It is a fascist ideal, however, because consistent with what occurred with both German Nazism and Italian fascism, Trump is very explicit in stating that the path to restoring lost greatness involves the displacement of certain 'undesirable' peoples already living in the United States (undocumented migrants, people on work visas, especially if they're from Middle Eastern countries) as well as the capture of lands beyond the borders (Canada, Greenland and so on). The displacement of 'undesirable' peoples is not restricted to foreign nationals living in the United States, the process is also directed at US citizens, particularly the already marginalized, such as the trans community, but also women seeking abortion, and the gay and lesbian community. Similarly, anything resembling 'welfare', or attempting to address 'equity' issues, is put on the chopping block and if not cut altogether then drastically curtailed, causing considerable disadvantage to millions of people, including many who voted for Trump. This combined with fantasies of a missile defence system (the 'Golden Dome') that seems to have been exhumed from Ronald Reagan's largely forgotten 'Star Wars' playbook and a relentless culture war aimed at everything progressive certainly adds up to a certain style of fascism. But as I said above, the real question is what kind of perversion of desire it entails.

To put in more specifically schizoanalytic terms: What is the nature of the plane of organization of our times such that someone like Trump, with all his many contradictions, could get elected? What abstract machine enabled him to become President? As Deleuze and Guattari put it, the abstract machine is said to play 'a piloting role', by which they mean it 'constructs a real that is yet to come, a new type of reality'.[28] In this sense, it can and I would suggest it should be understood as playing a role not unlike that of the aesthetic category. As Sianne Ngai shows, aesthetic categories attract, give shape to and reward our desire by focalizing it in determinate ways and by policing the boundaries. Its agency extends well beyond a single text, indeed its real power is demonstrated in the way it connects a multiplicity of texts at the level of their design idea, impetus and inspiration. Modernism, which spanned architecture, fashion, painting, literature, music and much else besides, exemplifies this point perfectly. This is why abstract machines always have a name and a date – they record the moment when a new way of thinking and seeing entered the world, rendering obsolete all existing assumptions about what is possible and impossible in a given field.[29] In this respect, the abstract machine bears an obvious resemblance to the notion of the event in that it demarcates a moment of transformation, but we need to take care here not to move too quickly and think of it solely in terms of its effects. The more important question, which Deleuze and Guattari spell out in their discussion of short stories and novellas, is this: 'Whatever could have happened?'[30] That is to say, whatever could have happened for this new way of thinking to have emerged?

The abstract machine does not 'stand outside history but is instead always "prior to" [*avant*] history.'[31] It exists as a virtual *but real* realm that invisibly, but nonetheless forcibly, presages the moment of an Absolute break with the existing order of things, without presenting itself as either a new form of infrastructure that is defining in the 'last instance' (Althusser) or the 'supreme instance' (Kant), or a cataclysmic fall into the chaotic or undifferentiated (Hegel).[32] Although specific historical conditions are necessary in an empirical sense for a particular abstract machine to emerge, the abstract machine is not born of those conditions, so it cannot be directly explained by those conditions. The abstract machine is always a leap in the dark. This is something art, which by its nature seeks to 'render visible' (as Deleuze and Guattari put it, borrowing from Paul Klee), can help us to understand.[33] But this phenomenon is by no means exclusive to art – it is to be found in the sciences, in politics, in architecture and so on. The question is always the same: Whatever could have happened for this artist, scientist, political thinker, architect and so on to have been able to see the world so differently? No one could have foreseen the artistic breaks Van Gogh, Picasso or even Warhol would make, probably not even the artists themselves, but when these breaks appeared they did so with the force and necessity of fate and the rigour of a category.

Irrespective of whether anyone appreciated their achievements, much less found their work appealing, Van Gogh, Picasso and Warhol sent shivers of possibility through the entire art world, opening up vistas no one had previously seen. If one takes a step back and asks what enabled these artists to create the works they did, when they did, under the conditions of their times, then the answer has to be not merely did they manage to see the world differently, but there existed, in virtual form, this other way of seeing the world that they were somehow able to tap into. In Van Gogh's case, in particular, the people who could appreciate his art were 'missing' until after many years after his death. The abstract machine names and theorizes this immanent but not-yet-realized potential to not merely see the world differently, but in a real sense to not see 'it' at all and instead see it as a disaggregated continuum of matter and function with infinite plastic potential.[34]

In artistic terms, one can envisage this as a set of unrealized possibilities, as the moment when in the artist's eyes all existing forms have dissolved and the new forms have not yet been brought into being but already their form can somehow be sensed but not known. There is nothing in classical painting that would allow us to predict the appearance of Picasso, nor is there anything in Picasso's work to explain *why* he departed from the classical artists he admired in the precise *way* that he did. This claim holds true even if one historicizes art and places it in the context of its own time – the grinding poverty of peasant life in Western Europe does not explain the appearance of Van Gogh's *Pair of Shoes*; if it did it might have sold in his lifetime instead of languishing like an old pair of shoes waiting for posterity to appreciate it. And though one may claim, as Jameson does, that the washed-out look of Warhol's *Diamond Dust Shoes* is a comment on the existential emptiness of late capitalism, one still cannot use the latter to *predict* the former.[35] The abstract machine of Picasso is not, however, cubism, or whatever artistic movement one wants to attach to his work, but rather the set of historical forces, by which I mean tensions in the collective state of desire, that enabled his work to be received as art. As much as Picasso admired Velasquez, one can imagine that Velasquez would not have admired Picasso, indeed in all likelihood Picasso's work would not have been regarded as art in the seventeenth century.

It is against this background question of what kind of abstract machine was required for Trump to become President that something like a Trump-assemblage becomes a useful concept because what it must explain is how and by what means it cuts across the multiple strata that would otherwise seem to be separated by culture, by tradition, by history, by belief, by political conviction and so on. Think of the Mexican man living on the US–Mexican border who voted for Trump: What calculation led to that choice when everything about his life would seem to point him elsewhere? There can be no illusion of false consciousness here. Trump was never shy or reticent in speaking about what he proposed to do that would directly affect the Latin American people living in the United States. The border wall Trump constantly boasted he'd build and get Mexico to pay for would separate him from his family and amplify the risks for other people hoping to cross the border too. Trump's inhuman policy of deporting undocumented migrants would also affect his community in detrimental ways. Trump also took every opportunity to stigmatize migrants, variously accusing them of stealing jobs, living on welfare, eating pets and so on. Given all this, how could a Mexican man vote for Trump? To answer this we need a more complex model of desire and its capacity to invest in antithetical ways.

Strata are part of the answer to that puzzle, but we also need the concept of the line. Strata are produced by processes Deleuze and Guattari refer to as 'coding' which is itself a codeword (i.e. translation) for 'repression', a word that they use freely in *Anti-Oedipus* but drop in *A Thousand Plateaus*. In contrast to Freud's notion of repression, though, Deleuze and Guattari theorize repression as something that desire desires.[36] Coding is one of the central operations of the assemblage and it occurs in two stages, which Deleuze and Guattari refer to as double articulation invoking the image of a lobster god: (1) selection, (2) consolidation. The most straightforward way to think about coding is in terms of group identity: for a group to exist as a group a certain set of differential criteria (e.g. distinguishing features) need to be identified that enable the selection of those who will belong to the group and those who will not. This is a process of coding because the features chosen only become significant because of the selection process – i.e. it is not the features that determine selection, but the other way round. For example, racial identity appears to be determined by skin colour, but there is no reason in principle why this feature of human identity should be significant. One can easily imagine a racially blind universe in which skin colour is utterly insignificant, of no more interest than whether someone has green or brown eyes. It is racism, as an assemblage, usually in the service of a higher power like capitalism or imperialism, that selects skin colour and mobilizes it as a group identity marker rendering it significant. The material existence of differently pigmented peoples is not by itself sufficient to have spawned racism – skin colour is merely available material for an exploitative assemblage looking to justify itself. This then is the second articulation, which Deleuze and Guattari characterize as a form of overcoding whereby the original coding process is made to seem to be 'naturally occurring'.[37]

People opposed to Trump perform what might called a form of 'counter-coding' inasmuch as they look for group identity makers that would seem to definitively separate Republican voters from Democrat voters. They tend to zero in on stupidity as though this is somehow a unique quality of Trump supporters, which of course it isn't. But what his detractors call stupidity is the seemingly inexplicable fact that many Trump supporters voted according to desire rather than interest. Stupidity can only be measured against interest, not desire. In this regard, Trump's detractors are on more solid ground when they point out the emphasis Trump's rhetoric places on masculinity because this is a matter of desire rather than interest. That being said, it raises as many questions as it answers: Why is masculinity so important to Trump voters? Under what conditions does masculinity become a matter of political concern? The Democrats didn't think it was significant enough to make it part of their platform, or rather they assumed that it would be so divisive it would hurt them at the polls. In their campaigning they focused almost exclusively on class interests, but by doing so they overlooked the way political desire works. As Cooper shows, the Republicans have been sowing the seeds of this particular political desire for many years by homing in on the way some men experience declining economic power as a form of feminization. This is a matter both of comparison with what men are earning in other industries and their sense that they could no longer support their families on a single wage.[38]

Masculinity as an election issue shifts the register from interest to desire and invites a very different set of calculations that do not always coincide with the voter's economic interest. Trump certainly created an atmosphere in which a particular variety of masculinity is emboldened to express itself and to act, but did not do anything to address the actual economic needs of these voters. Trump capitalized on a political fault line that according to Cooper first made its appearance with the so-called Tax Revolt in California in 1978 which led to the infamous Proposition 13 that simultaneously capped the amount of property tax that could be levied by the state and made it all but impossible for future legislators to alter this situation. Its effect was to drastically reduce the amount of funding the state had at its disposal to provide services, such as schools.

This drop in state spending on services particularly impacted poorer neighbourhoods, which generally have a predominantly 'non-white' population, where residents were unable to afford the cost of private services. As Cooper points out, wealthier people, typically white, also experienced a generalized reduction in the provision of government services, but they were able to compensate by using private services. As such, she argues, they effectively voted against their own apparent interests 'in order to disenfranchise Blacks in particular'.[39] Interest, in other words, is not a reliable guide to political choices – people frequently vote against their interests in the name of desire. This is not to say that by contrast desire is a reliable guide, clearly it isn't. Rather, what it points to is the need to treat desire as a complex multiplicity consisting of a variety of different moving parts.

Let us turn now to the plane of immanence which, as I mentioned above, is principally subdivided into lines. The notion of the line is central to the whole schizoanalytic project, but the word itself does not come into use until the publication of *A Thousand Plateaus*. It doesn't feature in *Anti-Oedipus* which instead uses the word 'flux', usually translated as 'flow' although this obscures the sense of disruption we associate with something being in a state of flux. Flows are fluctuations in affect. *A Thousand Plateaus* replaces the word 'flow' with 'line', but the object remains the same: fluctuations in affect. Deleuze and Guattari do not specify a single source for the notion of line they mobilize – it is linked to cartography, topography, topology, music, painting and so on. No explanation is given for the change in terminology, but I suspect it has to do with the fact their use of flow is tied to material flows, such as bodily fluids, and this ultimately proved limiting for the work they were trying to do. Lines, by contrast, which are obviously more abstract than flows, have considerably more versatility from a schematic perspective, and that seems to have suited them better as they developed the second part of their project. Where strata is a figuration of discrete layers of grouped and directly connected elements, the line is a figuration of superlinear connections that cut across groups. The line represents the ever-present possibility of both the disintegration of the group, either all at once or bit by bit, and the formation of a new group. If we refer back to the example of masculinity this can be illustrated as follows. Masculinity is a line that cuts across the strata of class interests linking men who otherwise have no common interests because they are separated by their socio-economic status, by the privileges and biases of race, by citizenship status and so on.

These men probably won't ever like each other or associate with each other because they remain so firmly within their own strata, but they nonetheless act in concert with one another at election time, thus forming a new group, namely Trump voters.

Masculinity functions as a relay switch, or what Deleuze and Guattari usefully call an assemblage converter, that causes desire and interest to become intertwined in such a way that interest is perceived through the lens of desire. In many ways, though, it is simply a screen for resentment, which following Cooper's insightful analysis of the so-called Tea Party revolt in the United States in the early 2000s we can define as *the overvaluation of perceived loss*. Sparked by the sub-prime loan meltdown that triggered the Global Financial Crisis of 2008 the Tea Party movement consisted of mostly older, mostly white, mostly middle-class people (small business owners rather than professionals) who were hit hard, but their losses were, as Cooper puts it, *relative rather than absolute*. Unlike the defaulting sub-prime mortgage holders they didn't lose their homes, or find themselves on the streets; rather, they experienced write-downs in the value of their homes – a paper loss not an actual loss – which restricted their borrowing capacity and impinged their lifestyle, and in some cases their pension funds shrank, but did not vanish; similarly, their businesses suffered, but they had the generous provisions of company bankruptcy law to cushion the blows, and unlike many they weren't rendered jobless and without income. They reeled from the loss of the 'wealth effect' they had hitherto enjoyed as an artefact of the housing boom which artificially pumped up the value of their home. They resented the interest rate hikes that were imposed to cool the housing market because they saw it as an impost they had to pay to subsidize people who weren't as financially 'responsible' as they felt they had been. In their fury against the government for, as they saw it, causing their financial difficulties, they railed against the government programmes such as the Affordable Care Act that actually helped them, but that they perceived to benefit the so-called undeserving poor. As was the case with the Tax Revolt they opposed government assistance in general, despite being long-time beneficiaries of government largesse in the form of tax concessions, in order to punish the poor in particular.[40]

These three examples – the Mexican Trump supporter, the California Tax Revolt and the Tea Party – are anything but exceptional in the way desire seems to short-circuit interest. At the heart of each of them is a contradiction between desire and interest that ideology is usually said to paper over by obscuring the real conditions of existence. This approach assumes that if people actually grasped the true nature of their situation they would think and act differently, but these examples suggest that we cannot be certain of that because desire rather than interest seems to have the upper hand in determining people's political choices. We cannot assume that if people realized that pushing for lower taxes would inevitably lead to a reduction of the provision of government services that they wouldn't still demand tax cuts. In all likelihood they would because they do not trust or believe in government and have bought into the neoliberal doctrine made famous in the Reagan era that private business provides better service. Ironically the many failures of private business to deliver programmes that government used to deliver has only tended to confirm the view that government shouldn't be trusted. It is in this context that anti-government politicians like Trump thrive – if government is the problem then getting rid of government is the solution, so the rhetoric goes. The problem is people still want and need the services government provides, indeed they generally want more of it not less, but they don't want to have to pay for it because they perceive others – i.e. the poor – to benefit more than they do. Because the poor seem to benefit more than they do, literally because they need more assistance than they do, the middle class perceive the taxes they pay as a loss, as an investment that failed to make a return. This feeling of resentment which drives their politics belongs to the order of desire, not interest, and it drives them to make transversal connections that cut across the strata and create new ways of thinking and seeing the world.

There is obviously a contradiction here between desire and interest, but it is not felt as such and as a consequence it doesn't need papering over with ideology. The question is, of course: How can one hold such opposing views without contradiction? Deleuze and Guattari acknowledge the inherent difficulty of answering this question when, as is the case in the example of housing booms, desire and interest are so intricately intertwined. 'It seems that schizoanalysis can make use only of indices – the machinic indices – in order to discern [. . .] the libidinal investments of the social field.'[41] Sexuality is one such index, but it is not the only one. Deleuze and Guattari also point us towards another set of more abstract indices that I believe offer a more useful framework for identifying the relevant indices of the libidinal investments of the social field. 'The fundamental difference between psychoanalysis and schizoanalysis is the following: schizoanalysis attains a non-figurative and non-symbolic unconscious, a pure abstract figural dimension ("abstract" in the sense of abstract painting), flow-schizzes or real desire, apprehended below the minimum conditions of identity.'[42] It is not our individual choices in life that define us – not our choice of lover, job, school, pastime and so on, all of these things are identifiable, they have distinct identities that we can recognize as interests. By themselves they are not indices. However, taken together they become indices because they prompt the question: By what subterranean means – rhizomes, magma flows, tunnels and so on (Deleuze and Guattari have always had a love of invisible connections) – are these choices connected? The indices of desire are to be found in the connections, disjunctions and conjunctions of flows that cut across a society linking past and present, present and future, old and new, and so on.

Today this approach to desire is to be found embedded in virtually every online recommendation algorithm. The central mission of every algorithm of this type is to figure out what combination of desiring-machines (these may be embodied in songs, books, cat videos, scented candles, etc.) a particular individual is interested in and likely to want to purchase. As Deleuze and Guattari in a sense predicted, algorithms are far more concerned with the 'and, and, and' than they are with 'is' – the analytic question they pose is: What can and cannot be accommodated in a string of conjunctions? As Deleuze and Guattari insist, all assemblages have cutting edges, which is to say there is always an internal structural limit to the 'and, and, and'. That limit is determined by the assemblage – but from an analytic perspective, the assemblage only becomes visible to us as an actual machine when we begin to ask what kinds of connections it mobilizes and what the limits are to those connections. We might assume that the Mexican man living on the US–Mexican border would have no interest in voting for Trump for all the good reasons I articulated above but we'd be wrong. One might say our error was to focus on 'is' – Mexican man living on the US–Mexican border – rather than the 'and, and, and' which would obviously give us very different picture. I have crudely – and I admit it's nothing more than a construct put together for heuristic purposes – added masculinity into the mix and argued that it effectively functions as what Deleuze and Guattari call an assemblage converter because against all odds it seems to induce the Mexican man living on the US–Mexican border to vote against his own interests and vote for someone who is demonstrably opposed to their very presence in the United States. The point I want to make here is this 'and, and, and' is a problem of the composition of affect because what is at stake is precisely the possibility of thinking and feeling antithetical desires without any sense of contradiction or conflict.

Finding the means of first of all modelling, then mapping, the connections, disjunctions and conjunctions of desire was, I would argue, the principal preoccupation of Deleuze and Guattari's entire collaboration. I am tempted to say it was an interest in the possibilities of cartography rather than politics that Guattari brought to his collaboration with Deleuze. It is a recurrent theme in Guattari's work but largely absent from Deleuze's with the exception of his work on Foucault whom he pointedly described as a cartographer. Where Deleuze and Guattari use the word 'map' they essentially mean some form of schema (to use an unfashionably Kantian term in a not necessarily Kantian way) that correlates to the non-empirical dimension of a given situation, or what I have in previous chapters referred to as the actual factors. Even if a given map accords a place for organic, ecological or technological elements, as Deleuze and Guattari say it should, the map itself does not refer to actual things in the world as the realists and vital materialists often insist. This is because, as Deleuze and Guattari clearly state in *What is Philosophy?*, the concept surveys only itself, there is no external point of reference, nothing that can in the last instance guarantee its validity. As Jameson puts it, schema are 'the X-ray of a concept; its premise being that, like an atom, a concept (whether scientific, ideological, philosophical, or even narrative) contains within itself smaller units and their relationships, which remain invisible to the naked eye'.[43] The schematic nature of Deleuze and Guattari's thinking is made manifest in the introduction to *A Thousand Plateaus* – literally on the first page – where it is said that a book is an assemblage and that as such, 'as in all things, there are lines of articulation or segmentarity, strata and territories; but also lines of flight, movements of deterritorialization and destratification. Comparative rates of flow on these lines produce phenomena of relative slowness and viscosity, or, on the contrary, of acceleration and rupture. All this, lines and measurable speeds, constitute an *assemblage*'.[44]

All of these cartographic features, as we may legitimately call them, are dimensions of either the plane of immanence (lines, flows, intensities, territories) or the plane of organization (segmentarities, strata), which is to say what they map is precisely the psychical agency of affect that has been our focus here. Taken together these features map the dynamic aspects of affect, accounting for its passions, its fixations, its lability, its capacity to compel us to think, perceive and feel. The mapping side of Deleuze and

Guattari's schizophrenic project is so prominent it tends to obscure the modelling side of it. Indeed, it has largely been the mapping side of things that has caught people's attention over the years – assemblages, rhizomes and lines of flight are all forms of mapping. However, as I have tried to demonstrate, the modelling side of their project is in many ways the most productive from an analytic perspective.

NOTES

Introduction

1 Gilles Deleuze, *Difference and Repetition* (p. xxi)

2 Jameson 1971: 183.

3 Deleuze 1989: 129.

4 Guattari 2016: 105.

5 Option 2 has been admirably documented and explored by Cross 2021.

6 Jameson 1981: 10.

7 Jameson 1972: 207.

8 Buchanan 2021a: 20.

9 Deleuze and Guattari 1986: 24.

10 Derrida 1976: 60.

11 Deleuze and Guattari 1987: 43.

12 Jameson 2007b: 151. Curiously, despite his reservations about Gramsci's strategy, Jameson holds out for the possibility of something similar to translation, which he calls 'transcoding' (borrowing the word from Deleuze and Guattari), 'and that is to deploy a language whose inner logic is precisely the suspension of the name and the holding open of the place for possibility, and that is the language of Utopia' (2009: 12). This is not the place to explore the implications of this notion, but given that Deleuze and Guattari are far from adverse to the language of Utopia I think it could be applied to their thought as well.

13 Benjamin 1968: 81.

14 Jameson 1990: 52.

15 Deleuze and Guattari 1994: 2.

16 Deleuze and Guattari 1994: 16.

17 Deleuze and Guattari 1994: 18.

18 The peoples we refer to as nomads did not bequeath us the concept, 'we' applied it to 'them', making them the bearers of 'our' ideas (including all 'our' misconceptions, prejudices and blindnesses). This is why the components of that concept – transversal movement and so on – can be applied to 'other' populations (e.g. artists, radical students, schizophrenics and so on).

19 Cited in Jameson 1991: 207.

20 On the problem of a natural language or plain language approach to reading Deleuze and Guattari, see my discussion of it in Buchanan 2021a: 19–20.

1 Schizoanalysis and Affect

1 Gilles Deleuze and Félix Guattari, *What is Philosophy?* (p. 83)

2 Deleuze and Guattari 1994: 83.

3 Massumi 2015: 92; Bennett 2010: 21.

4 Deleuze and Guattari 1994: 16.

5 Deleuze 1995: 144.

6 Deleuze 1995: 145.

7 Deleuze 1995: 145.

8 Deleuze 1995: 152.

9 Deleuze 1995: 152.

10 Deleuze 1995: 153. It is worth noting here that Deleuze's objection to the incipient form of the European Union for being overly technocratic (Deleuze 1995: 172) follows exactly the same line of attack as new left scholars like Perry Anderson (2021), who rejected Deleuze and Guattari's work as irrational.

11 Deleuze 1995: 153.

12 Deleuze 1995: 153, emphasis added.

13 Deleuze 2006: 88.

14 Deleuze 2006: 88.

15 Buchanan 2021a: 61; 2008: 59.

16 Deleuze 2004: 269.

17 Deleuze

18 DeLanda 1997: 281 n.12.

19 Jameson 1971: 74. To which one may add Fressoz's incisive judgement that materialist theories of the DeLanda type are actually 'inspired by idealist philosophies of history' (2024: 39).

20 Massumi 2002: 24.

21 Jameson 1971: 185.

22 Jameson 1971: 186.

23 The situation in affect theory is complicated by the fact that the work of Silvan Tomkins is also recognized as an important starting point, but looking at the early work in the field it appears that affect theory was already in motion when Tomkins's work was picked up. For instance, in an essay introducing Tomkins's work, published in 2003, Eve Kosofsky Sedgwick and Adam Frank noted that his work was 'not presently well-known' (p. 94).

24 De Certeau 1984: 62–3.

25 Deleuze 1994: 129.

26 Deleuze and Parnet 2007: 28.

27 Deleuze 1995: 25.

28 Deleuze 1995: 25.

29 Borges 1970: 236.

30 Deleuze and Guattari 1994: 51.

31 In this respect I take a very different course from Donald Cross (2021) in his excellent book *Deleuze and the Problem of Affect*, which is certainly the most comprehensive account we have of the many iterations of affect to be found in Deleuze and Guattari.

32 Deleuze and Guattari 1987: 10.

33 Deleuze and Guattari 1983: 29.

34 Deleuze 1997: 126

35 Deleuze and Guattari 1994: 67.

36 Deleuze 1994: xxi.

37 Deleuze 1994: xxii.

38 Deleuze 1994: xix.

39 Hemmings 2005: 556.

40 Leys 2017: 312 n.13.

41 Leys 2017: 313. See, for example, Massumi's discussion of EEG machines in 'The Autonomy of Affect' (2002: 29).

42 Papoulias and Callard 2010: 51 n.3.

43 Gregg and Seigworth 2010: 6; Clough 2007.

44 Hemmings 2005: 553.

45 Probyn 2010: 76.

46 Massumi 2002: 27.

47 Massumi 2002: 32–3.

48 Massumi 2002: 32–3.

49 Leys 2017: 313; Brinkema 2014: 270 n.62.

50 Massumi 2015: 4.

51 Massumi 2015: 94.

52 Massumi 2015: 94.

53 Massumi 2015: 94–5, emphasis in original.

54 Massumi 2015: 95.

55 Massumi 2015: 3.

56 Massumi 2015: 4.

57 Massumi 2015: 91.

58 Massumi is presumably not unaware of this, given that a few pages later he explicitly discusses Deleuze's account of 'reactive forces' in Nietzsche, which only makes this claim all the more mystifying (2015: 103).

59 Massumi 2015: 92.

60 Sacks 2012: 66.

2 Overwhelmed by Desire

1 Gilles Deleuze, *Negotiations* (p. 136)

2 Deleuze and Guattari 1987: 161.

3 Deleuze and Guattari 1983: 133.

4 Deleuze and Guattari 1994: 218, emphasis in original.

5 Deleuze 1997: 3.

6 Cited in Thaventhiran 2024: 30.

7 Deleuze and Guattari 1987: 302.

8 Spinoza 1994: 77.

9 Deleuze and Guattari 1987: 248.

10 Deleuze and Guattari 1987: 283.

11 Deleuze and Guattari 1987: 285.

12 Deleuze and Guattari 1987: 166.

13 Guattari 1995: 177–85.

14 This section builds on work undertaken in Buchanan 2021a and 2021b.

15 Deleuze and Guattari 1983: 9.

16 Deleuze and Guattari 1983: 42.

17 Deleuze and Guattari 1983: 29, emphasis in original.

18 Deleuze and Guattari 1983: 24.

19 Deleuze and Guattari 1983: 27.

20 Deleuze and Guattari 1994: 42.

21 Deleuze and Guattari 1987: 7.

22 Deleuze and Guattari 1987: 14.

23 Deleuze and Guattari 1987: 251.

24 Deleuze and Guattari 1983: 66.

25 Deleuze 1990: 189. See also Buchanan 2021a: 49.

26 Deleuze and Guattari 1983: 329.

27 Deleuze and Guattari 1983: 8.

28 Deleuze and Guattari 1983: 8.

29 Deleuze and Guattari 1983: 35.

30 Deleuze and Guattari 1987: 229.

31 Deleuze 1989: 172, emphasis in original.

32 Deleuze and Guattari 1983: 78.

33 Deleuze and Guattari 1983: 25.

34 Deleuze and Guattari 1983: 25.

35 Deleuze and Guattari 1983: 25.

36 Deleuze 1994: 58.

37 Deleuze 1994: 58.

38 Deleuze 1994: 87.

39 Deleuze 1994: 98.

40 Deleuze 1994: 98.

41 Foucault 1970: xv.

42 Deleuze 1994: 148.

43 Deleuze and Guattari 1983: 26.

44 Deleuze and Guattari 1983: 26.

45 De Certeau 1986: 191.

46 Deleuze 1994: 56-57.

47 Deleuze 1994: 57.

48 Deleuze 1994: 79.

49 Deleuze and Guattari 1983: 3.

50 Deleuze and Guattari 1983: 8.

51 Thornton 2025: 174.

52 Deleuze and Guattari 1983: 8.

53 Deleuze and Guattari 1983: 8.

54 Deleuze and Guattari 1983: 8.

55 Deleuze and Guattari 1983: 8.

56 Deleuze and Guattari 1987: 38.

57 Deleuze and Guattari 1983: 15.

58 Deleuze and Guattari 1983: 8.

59 Deleuze and Guattari 1983: 9.

60 Deleuze and Guattari 1983: 13.

61 Deleuze and Guattari 1983: 11.

62 Deleuze and Guattari 1987: 150.

63 Buchanan 2021a: 75–84.

64 Deleuze and Guattari 1987: 152.

65 Deleuze and Guattari 1987: 155.

66 Deleuze and Guattari 1987: 155.

67 Deleuze and Guattari 1987: 154.

68 Deleuze and Guattari 1983: 10.

69 Deleuze and Guattari 1983: 10.

70 It is a *spatium*: 'It is not space, nor is it in space; it is matter that *occupies* space to a given degree – to the degree corresponding to the intensities produced" (Deleuze and Guattari 1987: 153, emphasis added). It should be noted that 'occupy' is the literal meaning of 'cathexis' (see Buchanan 2021a: 61).

71 Dick 1997 [1968]: 9.

72 Deleuze and Guattari 1987: 183.

73 Deleuze and Guattari 1987: 179.

74 Berlant 2011: 1.

3 *That* Plane Works for Me

1 Gilles Deleuze and Félix Guattari, *A Thousand Plateaus* (p. 235)

2 Deleuze and Guattari 1983: 3.

3 Cited in Deleuze and Guattari 1983: 11.

4 As I shown elsewhere, the word 'invest' here is a translation of 'investissement', which in turn is the French rendering of Freud's term *Besetzung*, that in English was rendered with the Greek word *cathexis* (Buchanan 2021a: 61).

5 DeLanda 2006: 20.

6 Deleuze and Guattari 1987: 283.

7 Primitive societies, as Deleuze and Guattari put it, were not unaware of exchange, or indeed markets, but they actively warded them off. Deleuze and Guattari 1983: 153, 156.

8 Jameson 2024.,

9 Jay and Scott 2023.

10 'No piece of coal or drop of fuel has yet turned itself into fuel, and no humans have engaged in systematic large-scale extraction of either to satisfy subsistence needs: fossil fuels necessitate waged or forced labour – the power of some to direct the labour of others – as conditions of their very existence' (Malm 2016: 19).

11 Deleuze and Guattari 1983: 197; Deleuze and Guattari 1987: 452.

12 Brown 2015: 28.

13 Deleuze 1988b: 33.

14 See Buchanan 2022.

15 Werrett 1999.

16 Cooper 2024: 375; Dardot and Laval 2019: xxiii.

17 Dardot and Laval 2019: 24.

18 Dardot and Laval 2019: 20.

19 Deleuze and Guattari 1987: 161.

20 Deleuze and Guattari 1987: 161.

21 Deleuze and Guattari 1987: 165.

22 Deleuze and Guattari 1987: 161.

23 Deleuze and Guattari 1987: 165.

24 Deleuze and Guattari 1987: 165.

25 Deleuze and Guattari 1987: 166, 286.

26 Deleuze and Guattari 1987: 157.

27 Deleuze and Parnet 2007: 34–5.

28 Deleuze and Guattari 1987: 252. Interestingly, there is an obvious echo here with the work of Jameson, who constantly insisted that we need to find strategies to totalize the situations we encounter. It also highlights the misunderstanding that many people seem to have regarding totalities, namely that they are somehow comparable with, or an index of, totalitarianism. This position was perhaps fomented by Lyotard and his call to wage war on totalities. But as Jameson always argued, totalization is simply our way of seeing the 'big picture', so it is an essential tool of critique.

29 Deleuze and Guattari 1987: 270.

30 Deleuze and Guattari 1987: 270.

31 Artaud cited in Deleuze and Guattari 1987: 160.

32 Foucault 1970: xv.

33 Foucault 1970: xv.

34 Foucault 1970: xvi–xvii.

35 Foucault 1970: xvii.

36 Deleuze and Guattari 1983: 77.

37 Carroll 1998: 15.

38 Deleuze and Guattari 1987: 240.

39 Deleuze and Guattari 1987: 240.

40 Nijinsky cited in Deleuze and Guattari 1983: 77.

41 Guattari 2013: 3.

42 See for example their discussion of Chomsky. Deleuze and Guattari 1987: 91–2.

43 Deleuze 2004.

44 Jameson 2024: 89. It should be noted my use of the terms 'diachronic' and 'synchronic' here and in what follows is derived from structural linguistics. It is in this regard very different from John Protevi's (2006) use of the same terms, which is drawn from complexity theory.

45 Fressoz 2024.

46 Jonathan Crary's *24/7* is an admiral attempt to depict the high energy consumption lifestyle in its full dystopian light.

47 It is my impression that Braudel is a far greater influence on DeLanda's conception of the assemblage than Deleuze and Guattari. This is not something one can necessarily prove, as it were, but it would certainly explain DeLanda's aversion to factoring desire into his accounts of historical change.

48 Gould 2000: 288.

49 Deleuze and Guattari 1987: 10.

50 Cited in Jameson 2024: 90.

51 Cited in Jameson 2024: 92.

4 Affect and Becoming

1 Gilles Deleuze and Félix Guattari, *What is Philosophy?* (p. 27)

2 Deleuze and Guattari 1987: 38.

3 Jameson 1991: 15.

4 Deleuze and Guattari 1987: 240.

5 Deleuze and Guattari 1987: 292.

6 Deleuze and Guattari 1987: 292.

7 Deleuze and Guattari 1987: 274.

8 Deleuze and Guattari take this example from Philippe Gavi.

9 Deleuze and Guattari 1987: 275.

10 Deleuze and Guattari 1987: 305.

11 Deleuze and Guattari 1987: 304.

12 Deleuze and Guattari 1994: 166, emphasis added.

14 Deleuze 1994: 139, emphasis added.

14 Deleuze 1994: 139.

15 Deleuze 1994: 139.

16 Deleuze 1994: 145.

17 Deleuze 1994: 146.

18 Deleuze 1984: xii.

19 Deleuze 1989: 157.

20 Deleuze 1994: 148.

21 Deleuze 1994: 146.

22 Deleuze 1994: 147.

23 Deleuze 1994: 147.

24 Deleuze and Guattari 1994: 42.

25 Deleuze and Guattari 1994: 54.

26 Deleuze and Guattari 1994: 54–5.

27 Deleuze and Guattari 1994: 55.

28 Deleuze and Guattari 1987: 240, emphasis in original.

29 Deleuze and Guattari 1987: 240.

30 Deleuze and Guattari 1987: 240, emphasis in original.

31 Deleuze and Guattari 1983: 18.

33 Deleuze and Guattari 1983: 18–19, emphasis added.

33 Jameson 1981: 23.

34 Deleuze and Guattari 1987: 27.

35 Deleuze and Guattari 1987: 27.

36 Deleuze and Guattari 1987: 27.

37 Deleuze and Guattari 1987: 28.

38 Deleuze and Guattari 1987: 239.

39 Deleuze and Guattari 1987: 245.

40 Deleuze and Guattari 1987: 32.

41 Deleuze and Guattari 1987: 245.

42 Deleuze and Guattari 1987: 27.

43 Deleuze and Guattari 1987: 240.

44 Buchanan 2008: 49.

45 Deleuze and Guattari 1987: 31.

46 Deleuze and Guattari 1987: 258.

47 Deleuze and Guattari 1987: 258.

48 Deleuze and Guattari 1987: 258, emphasis added.

49 Deleuze and Guattari 1987: 258.

50 Deleuze and Guattari 1987: 259.

51 Deleuze and Guattari 1983: 35; 1987: 229.

52 Deleuze and Guattari 1987: 155.

53 Deleuze and Guattari 1987: 257.

54 Deleuze and Guattari 1987: 257.

55 Deleuze and Guattari 1987: 258.

56 Deleuze and Guattari 1987: 258.

57 Deleuze and Guattari 1987: 258.

58 Deleuze 1992: 220.

59 Deleuze 1992: 219.

60 Deleuze and Guattari 1987: 257. See also Deleuze 1988a: 124–5.

61 Deleuze and Guattari 1987: 256.

62 Deleuze and Guattari 1987: 256.

63 Deleuze and Guattari 1987: 153.

64 Deleuze and Guattari 1987: 162.

65 Deleuze and Guattari 1987: 156.

66 Deleuze and Guattari 1987: 395.

67 Deleuze and Guattari 1987: 395, emphasis added.

68 Deleuze and Guattari 1987: 395.

69 Deleuze and Guattari 1987: 396.

70 Deleuze and Guattari 1987: 396.

71 Deleuze and Guattari 1987: 397.

72 Deleuze and Guattari 1987: 396, emphasis added.

73 Deleuze and Guattari 1987: 395, emphasis added.

74 Buchanan 2021a: 122–32.

75 Deleuze and Guattari 1987: 395.

76 Deleuze and Guattari 1987: 397.

77 Deleuze and Guattari 1987: 397.

78 Deleuze and Guattari 1987: 397.

79 Deleuze and Guattari 1987: 398.

80 Deleuze and Guattari 1987: 400.

81 Deleuze and Guattari 1987: 400.

5 Modelling Affect

1 Gilles Deleuze and Félix Guattari, *Anti-Oedipus* (p. 151)

2 Sartre 1986: 14.

3 In an ironic twist, the person who formulated in philosophical terms the notion of 'let die' in the most coherent way, Giorgio Agamben, turned out to be one of the most vocal opponents of public health strategies (face masks, vaccines, quarantines, etc.) intended to prevent people from being let to die. A collection of his 'op eds' have been published in English as *Where Are We Now? The Epidemic as Politics?* The paranoid tone of these pieces raises a very interesting question: is his concept of bare life paranoid in its construction too? This question is out of scope of this project, but as a long-time reader of Agamben I'll admit it troubles me.

4 Cooper 2024: 190.

5 Cooper 2024: 107–95.

6 Deleuze and Guattari 1983: 29.

7 Corey Robin has argued convincingly that Trump's politics should not be regarded as fascistic. While largely agreeing with his argument, I tend to take a more expansive approach in my understanding of fascism, and in broad agreement with Toscano's approach in *Late Fascism* think there is tutelary value in so naming it. Robin 2018: 264–9.

8 Deleuze and Guattari 1983: 29.

9 Deleuze and Guattari 1983: 344; Deleuze and Guattari 1987: 68.

10 Jameson's *Marxism and Form*, which was published in 1971, offers ample of evidence of the variety of different ways ideology has been conceived by the Marxist tradition at that time.

11 The concept of 'net zero' emissions is perhaps the most pernicious example of 'false consciousness' at work because it glosses over the fact that carbon capture does not occur at the same rate as carbon emission. It also ignores the fact that we have already passed several tipping points that have put us on a path to an increase in global temperature that many scientists believe will be catastrophic.

12 Deleuze 1995: 18–19.

13 Dardot and Laval 2013: 86.

14 Cooper 2024: 169–70.

15 Deleuze and Guattari 1983: 350, emphasis added.

16 Jameson 1991: 69.

17 Deleuze 1989: 221.

18 Deleuze 1989: 221–2.

19 Jameson 1994: 44.

20 Deleuze and Guattari 1986: 16–17.

21 Deleuze and Guattari 1983: 42.

22 Deleuze and Guattari 1983: 42.

23 Jameson 2009: 410.

24 Fitzgerald 1956: 69.

25 Foucault 1981: 51.

26 Deleuze and Guattari 1987: 151.

27 Deleuze and Guattari 1987: 151.

28 Deleuze and Guattari 1987: 142.

29 Deleuze and Guattari 1987: 142.

30 Deleuze and Guattari 1987: 192.

31 Deleuze and Guattari 1987: 142.

32 Deleuze and Guattari 1987: 142.

33 Deleuze and Guattari 1987: 342.

34 Deleuze and Guattari 1987: 141.

35 Jameson 1991: 8–10.

36 Deleuze and Guattari 1983: 32.

37 Deleuze and Guattari 1987: 41.

38 Cooper 2024: 132–7.

39 Cooper 2024: 223.

40 Cooper 2024: 177–80.

41 Deleuze and Guattari 1983: 350.

42 Deleuze and Guattari 1983: 351.

43 Jameson 2023: 31.

44 Deleuze and Guattari 1987: 3–4.

BIBLIOGRAPHY

Anderson, P. 2021 *Ever Closer the Union? Europe in the West*, London: Verso.

Adkins, B. 2015 *Deleuze and Guattari's A Thousand Plateaus: A Critical Introduction and Guide*, Edinburgh: Edinburgh University Press.

Agamben, G. 1993 *The Coming Community*, trans M. Hardt, Minneapolis: University of Minnesota Press.

Artaud, A. 1976 *Antonin Artaud: Selected Writings*, trans H. Weaver, Berkeley: University of California Press.

Attali, J. 1985 *Noise: The Political Economy of Music*, trans B. Massumi, Minneapolis: University of Minnesota Press.

Barad, K. 2007 *Meeting the Universe Halfway: Quantum Physics and the Entanglement of Matter and Meaning*, Durham, NC: Duke University Press.

Barthes, R. 1989 *The Rustle of Language*, trans R. Howard, Berkeley: University of California Press.

Barthes, R. 1982 *Camera Obscura*, trans R. Howard, London: Jonathan Cape.

Barthes, R. 1977 *Image, Music, Text*, trans S. Heath, London: Fontana Press.

Barthes, R. 1972 *Mythologies*, trans A. Lavers, London: Paladin.

Benjamin, W. 1968 *Illuminations: Essays and Reflections*, trans H. Zohn, New York: Schocken Books.

Bennett, J. 2010 *Vibrant Matter: A Political Ecology of Things*, Durham, NC: Duke University Press.

Bennett, J. 2001 *The Enchantment of Modern Life: Attachments, Crossings, and Ethics*, Princeton: Princeton University Press.

Berlant, L. 2011 *Cruel Optimism*, Durham, NC: Duke University Press.

Borges, J. 1970 *Labyrinths*, ed D. Yates and J. Irby, London: Penguin.

Brinkema, E. 2014 *The Forms of Affects*, Durham, NC: Duke University Press.

Brown, W. 2015 *Undoing the Demos: Neoliberalism's Stealth Revolution*, New York: Zone Books.

Brown, W. 1995 *States of Injury: Power and Freedom in Late Modernity*, Princeton: Princeton University Press.

Buchanan, I. 2022 'Biopolitics, Discipline and Governmentality' in S. S. Das and A. R. Pratihar (eds) *Technology, Urban Space and the Networked Community*, New York: Palgrave, pp 1–28.

Buchanan, I. 2021a *Assemblage Theory and Method*, London: Bloomsbury.

Buchanan, I. 2021b *The Incomplete Project of Schizoanalysis: Collected Essays on Deleuze and Guattari*, Edinburgh: Edinburgh University Press.

Buchanan, I. 2019 'Must we eat fish?', *Symploke* 27: 1–2, pp 79–90.

Buchanan, I. 2008 *A Reader's Guide to Anti-Oedipus*, London: Bloomsbury.

Buchanan, I. 2006 *Fredric Jameson: Live Theory*, London: Bloomsbury.

Buchanan, I. 2000 *Deleuzism: A Metacommentary*, Durham, NC: Duke University Press.

Butler, J. 2015 *Senses of the Subject*, New York: Fordham University Press.

Carroll, L. 1998 *Alice's Adventures in Wonderland*, London: Penguin.

Clark, T. J. 2022 *If These Apples Should Fall: Cézanne and the Present*, London: Thames & Hudson.

Clough, P. (ed) 2007 *The Affective Turn: Theorizing the Social*, Durham, NC: Duke University Press.

Cooper, M. 2024 *Counterrevolution: Extravagance and Austerity in Public Finance*, New York: Zone Books.

Crary, J. 2001 *Suspensions of Perception: Attention, Spectacle, and Modern Culture*, Cambridge, MA: MIT Press.

Cross, D. 2021 *Deleuze and the Problem of Affect*, Edinburgh: Edinburgh University Press.

de Certeau, M. 1986 *Heterologies: Discourse on the Other*, trans B. Massumi, Minneapolis: University of Minnesota Press.

de Certeau, M. 1984 *The Practice of Everyday life*, trans S. Rendall, Berkeley: The University of California Press.

Dardot, P. and Laval, C. 2019 *Never-Ending Nightmare: The Neo-Liberal Assault on Democracy*, trans G. Elliott, London: Verso.

Dardot, P. and Laval, C. 2013 *The New Way of the World: On Neo-Liberal Society*, trans G. Elliott, London: Verso.

DeLanda, M. 2006 *A New Philosophy of Society: Assemblage Theory and Social Complexity*, London: Continuum.

DeLanda, M. 1997 *A Thousand Years of Nonlinear History*, New York: Zone Books.

Deleuze, G. 2006 *Two Regimes of Madness: Texts and Interviews 1975–1995*, trans A. Hodges and M. Taormina, New York: Semiotext(e).

Deleuze, G. 2004 *Desert Islands and Other Texts 1953–1974*, trans M. Taormina, New York: Semiotext(e).

Deleuze, G. 2003 *Francis Bacon: The Logic of Sensation*, trans D. Smith, London: Continuum.

Deleuze, G. 2000 *Proust and Signs*, trans R. Howard, Minneapolis: University of Minnesota Press.

Deleuze, G. 1997 *Essays Critical and Clinical*, trans D. Smith and M. Greco, Minneapolis: University of Minnesota Press.

Deleuze, G. 1995 *Negotiations*, trans M. Joughin, New York: Columbia University Press.

Deleuze, G. 1994 *Difference and Repetition*, trans P. Patton, London: Athlone Press.

Deleuze, G. 1992 *Expressionism in Philosophy: Spinoza*, trans M. Joughin, New York: Zone Books.

Deleuze, G. 1991 *Empiricism and Subjectivity: An Essay on Hume's Theory of Human Nature*, trans C. Boundas, New York: Columbia University Press.

Deleuze, G. 1990 *The Logic of Sense*, trans M. Lester, London: Athlone Press.

Deleuze, G. 1989 *Cinema 2: The Time-Image*, trans H. Tomlinson and R. Galeta, Minneapolis: University of Minnesota Press.

Deleuze, G. 1988a *Spinoza: Practical Philosophy*, trans R. Hurley, San Francisco: City Light Books.

Deleuze, G. 1988b *Foucault*, trans S. Hand, Minneapolis: University of Minnesota Press.

Deleuze, G. 1986 *Cinema 1: The Movement-Image*, trans H. Tomlinson and B. Habberjam, Minneapolis: University of Minnesota Press.

Deleuze, G. 1984 *Kant's Critical Philosophy: The Doctrine of the Faculties*, trans H. Tomlinson and B. Habberjam, London: Athlone Press.

Deleuze, G. 1983 *Nietzsche and Philosophy*, trans H. Tomlinson, London: Athlone Press.

Deleuze, G. and Guattari, F. 1994 *What is Philosophy?* trans H. Tomlinson and G. Burchell, New York: Columbia University Press.

Deleuze, G. and Guattari, F. 1987 *A Thousand Plateaus: Capitalism and Schizophrenia*, trans B. Massumi, Minneapolis: University of Minnesota Press.

Deleuze, G. and Guattari, F. 1986 *Kafka: Toward a Minor Literature*, trans D. Polan, Minneapolis: University of Minnesota Press.

Deleuze, G. and Guattari, F. 1983 *Anti-Oedipus: Capitalism and Schizophrenia*, trans R. Hurley et al, Minneapolis: University of Minnesota Press.

Deleuze, G. and Parnet, C. 2007 *Dialogues II* (revised edition), trans H. Tomlinson and B. Habberjam, New York: Columbia University Press.

Dick, P. K. 1997 *Do Androids Dream of Electric Sheep?* London: HarperCollins.

Dienst, R. 1995 *Still Life in Real Time: Theory After Television*, Durham, NC: Duke University Press.

Derrida, J. 1976 *Of Grammatology*, trans G. Spivak, Baltimore: Johns Hopkins University Press.

Durand, C. 2024 *How Silicon Valley Unleashed Techno-Feudalism*, trans D. Broder, London: Verso.

Eco, U. 1979 *The Role of the Reader: Explorations in the Semiotics of Texts*, Bloomington: Indiana University Press.

Eubanks, V. 2017 *Automating Inequality: How High-Tech Tools Profile, Police, and Punish the Poor*, New York: St. Martin's Press.

Fitzgerald, F. S. 1956 *The Crack-Up*, New York: New Directions.

Foucault, M. 2008 *The Birth of Biopolitics: Lectures at the College de France 1978-1979*, trans G. Burchell, New York: Palgrave.

Foucault, M. 1981 'The Order of Discourse' in R. Young, *Untying the Text Poststructuralist Reader*, London: Routledge, pp 51–78.

Foucault, M. 1980 *Language, Counter-Memory, Practice: Selected Essays and Interviews*, trans D. Bouchard and S. Simon, Ithaca, NY: Cornell University Press.

Foucault, M. 1978 *The History of Sexuality: An Introduction*, trans R. Hurley, London: Penguin.

Foucault, M. 1977 *Discipline and Punish: The Birth of the Modern Prison*, trans A. Sheridan, London: Penguin.

Foucault, M. 1972 *The Archaeology of Knowledge*, trans A. M. Sheridan Smith, London: Tavistock.

Foucault, M. 1970 *The Order of Things*, London: Tavistock.

Freud, S. 1984 *On Metapsychology: The Theory of Psychoanalysis*, trans J. Strachey, London: Penguin.

Freud, S. 1976 *The Interpretation of Dreams*, trans J. Strachey, London: Penguin.

Fressoz, J.-B. 2024 *More and More and More: An All-Consuming History of Energy*, London: Allen Lane.

Gould, S. J. 2000 *Wonderful Life: The Burgess Shale and the Nature of History*, London: Vintage.

Gregg, M. and Seigworth, G. (eds) 2010 *The Affect Theory Reader*, Durham, NC: Duke University Press.

Guattari, F. 2016 *Lines of Flight: For Another World of Possibilities*, trans A. Goffey, London: Bloomsbury.

Guattari, F. 2013 *Schizoanalytic Cartographies*, trans A. Goffey, London: Bloomsbury.

Guattari, F. 1996a *Soft Subversions*, trans D. Sweet and C. Wiener, New York: Semiotext(e).

Guattari, F. 1996b *The Guattari Reader*, ed G. Genosko, Oxford: Blackwell.

Guattari, F. 1995 *Chaosophy*, ed S. Lotringer, New York: Semiotext(e).

Guattari, F. 1984 *The Molecular Revolution: Psychiatry and Politics*, trans R. Sheed, London: Penguin.

Hemmings, C. 2005 'Invoking Affect: Cultural Theory and the Ontological Turn', *Cultural Studies* 19: 5, pp 548–67.

Hickey-Moody, A. 2019 *Deleuze and Masculinity*, London: Palgrave.

Jameson, F. 2024 *The Years of Theory: Postwar French Thought to the Present*, London: Verso.

Jameson, F. 2023 'Schematizations, or How to Draw a Thought', *Critical Inquiry* 50: 1, pp 31–53.

Jameson, F. 2019 *Allegory and Ideology*, London: Verso.

Jameson, F. 2018 'Itemized', *London Review of Books*, 8 November 2022.

Jameson, F. 2013 *The Antinomies of Realism*, London: Verso.

Jameson, F. 2009 *Valences of the Dialectic*, London: Verso.

Jameson, F. 2007a *The Modernist Papers*, London: Verso.

Jameson, F. 2007b *Jameson on Jameson: Conversations on Cultural Marxism*, Durham, NC: Duke University Press.

Jameson, F. 2003 'The End of Temporality', *Critical Inquiry* 29: 4, pp 695–718.

Jameson, F. 1994 *The Seeds of Time*, New York: Columbia University Press.

Jameson, F. 1991 *Postmodernism, or, The Cultural Logic of Late Capitalism*, London: Verso.

Jameson, F. 1990 *Late Marxism: Adorno, or, The Persistence of the Dialectic*, London: Verso.

Jameson, F. 1981 *The Political Unconscious: Narrative as a Socially Symbolic Act*, London: Routledge.

Jameson, F. 1972 *The Prison-House of Language: A Critical Account of Structuralism and Russian Formalism*, Princeton: Princeton University Press.

Jameson, F. 1971 *Marxism and Form: Twentieth-Century Dialectical Theories of Literature*, Princeton: Princeton University Press.

Jay, S. and Acott, T. 2023 '"Tussling with seascape character assessment and assemblage theories', *Journal of Environmental Policy & Planning* 10.1080/1523908X.2023.2251905

Latour, B. 2005 *Reassembling the Social: An Introduction to Actor-Network-Theory*, Oxford: Oxford University Press.

Leys, R. 2017 *The Ascent of Affect: Genealogy and Critique*, Chicago: University of Chicago Press.

Lordon, F. 2014 *Willing Slaves of Capital: Spinoza and Marx on Desire*, trans G. Ash, London: Verso.

MacKenzie, D. 2024 'Hey Big Spender', *London Review of Books*, 15 August.

Malm, A. 2018 *The Progress of this Storm: Nature and Society in a Warming World*, London: Verso.

Malm, A. 2016 *Fossil Capital: The Rise of Steam Power and the Roots of Global Warming*, London: Verso.

Massumi, B. 2015 *Politics of Affect*, London: Polity Press.

Massumi, B. 2002 *Parables of the Virtual: Movement, Affect, Sensation*, Durham, NC: Duke University Press.

Massumi, B. 1992 *A User's Guide to Capitalism and Schizophrenia: Deviations from Deleuze and Guattari*, Cambridge, MA: MIT Press.

Meek, J, 2024 'Market Forces and Malpractice', *London Review of Books*, 4 July, pp 9–16.

Noble, S. 2018 *Algorithms of Oppression: How Search Engines Reinforce Racism*, New York: NYU Press.

Papoulias, C. and Callard, F. 2010 'Biology's Gift: Interrogating the Turn to Affect', *Body and Society* 16: 1, pp 29–56.

Pettman, D. 2016 *Infinite Distraction: Paying Attention to Social Media*, London: Polity Press.

Prideaux, S. 2005 *Edvard Munch: Behind the Scream*, New Haven: Yale University Press.

Probyn, E. 2010 'Writing Shame' in M. Gregg and G. Seigworth (eds) *The Affect Theory Reader*, Durham, NC: Duke University Press, pp 71–90.

Protevi, J. 2006 'Deleuze, Guattari and Emergence', *Paragraph* 29: 2, pp 19–39.

Robin, C. 2018 *The Reactionary Mind: Conservatism from Edmund Burke to Donald Trump*, New York: Oxford University Press.

Sacks, O. 2012 *Hallucinations*, London: Picador.

Sartre, J.-P. 1986 [1945] *The Reprieve*, trans E. Sutton, London: Penguin.

Savage, G. 2020 'What is policy assemblage?', *Territory, Politics, Governance* 8: 3, pp 319–35.

Seaver, N. 2022 *Computing Taste: Algorithms and the Makers of Music Recommendations*, Chicago: University of Chicago Press.

Sedgwick, E. K. 2003 *Touching Feeling: Affect, Pedagogy, Feeling*, Durham, NC: Duke University Press.

Spinoza, B. 1994 *Ethics*, trans E. Curley, London: Penguin.

Srnicek, N. 2017 *Platform Capitalism*, Cambridge: Polity Press.

Streeck, W. 2016 *How Will Capitalism End? Essays on a Failing System*, London: Verso.

Tarnoff, B. 2022 *Internet for the People: The Fight for Our Digital Future*, London: Verso.

Thaventhiran, H. 2024 'No Dose for it at the Chemist', *London Review of Books*, 24 October, pp 29–32.

Wacquant, L. 2009 *Punishing the Poor: The Neoliberal Government of Social Insecurity*, Durham, NC: Duke University Press.

Werrett, S. 1999 'Potemkin and the Panopticon: Samuel Bentham and the Architecture of Absolutism in Eighteenth Century Russia', *Journal of Bentham Studies* 2: 1, pp 1–25.

Williams, R. 1974 *Television: Technology and Cultural Form*, London: Fontana.

Žižek, S. 1989 *The Sublime Object of Ideology*, London: Verso.

Zuboff, S. 2019 *The Age of Surveillance Capitalism: The Fight for a Human Future at the Frontier of Power*, London: Profile.